Regreen

Regreen
New Canadian Ecological Poetry

edited by
Madhur Anand and Adam Dickinson

Your Scrivener Press

Library and Archives Canada Cataloguing in Publication

    Regreen : new Canadian ecological poetry / editors: Madhur Anand and Adam Dickinson.

ISBN 978-1-896350-36-3

    1. Canadian poetry (English)—20th century. 2. Canadian poetry (English)—21st century. 3. Nature—Poetry. 4. Ecology—Poetry. I. Anand, Madhur, 1971- II. Dickinson, Adam, 1974-

PS8287.N38R43 2009   C811'.5408036   C2009-904232-0

Book design: Laurence Steven
Cover design: Chris Evans

Published by Your Scrivener Press
465 Loach's Road,
Sudbury, Ontario, Canada, P3E 2R2
info@yourscrivenerpress.com
www.yourscrivenerpress.com

We acknowledge the support of the Canada Council for the Arts and the Ontario Arts Council for our publishing program.

Canada Council   Conseil des Arts   ONTARIO ARTS COUNCIL
for the Arts   du Canada   CONSEIL DES ARTS DE L'ONTARIO

Contents

Introductions

ADAM DICKINSON   The Astronauts   9
MADHUR ANAND   Gap Dynamics   19

• a triumph of tubers •

RHEA TREGEBOV   Elegy for the Wild   30

MAUREEN SCOTT HARRIS   Be the River   31

BERT ALMON   Duty of Care   32

CORNELIA HOOGLAND   the Science (and poetry) of what's
hard-wired   34
The Story of Art   36

ALANNA F. BONDAR   What in the tall trees? Stacks made
for undoing & leaves the
shape of reaching   37

MONIQUE CHÉNIER   Falconbridge 1964-1975   41

JAN CONN   Monsoon, Early June   43
Animated Plants   44

RUTH ROACH PIERSON   A scree of crystalline blisters   45
Heat wave   47

BRIAN BARTLETT   Leaving the Island   48

ROBYN SARAH   As a storm-lopped tree   50
For Light   51
Gate   52

ARMAND GARNET RUFFO   Ethic   53
Sudbury, Night   54

DON MCKAY   from *The Muskwa Assemblage*   55

• pristine modernity, the dream •

KAREN HOULE   In the eighth   59

RHONDA COLLIS   Sudbury – 1972   61

MARI-LOU ROWLEY   In the Tar Sands, Going Down   63

JANE MUNRO   Do not exult yourself   67
                         Like the moon, come out from
                              behind the clouds. Shine!   68

OLIVE SENIOR   Greenhorn   70

SINA QUEYRAS   Cloverleaf, medians & means   71

RITA WONG   resilience, impure, forms   76
                         resuscitate   77
                         green trust   78
                         return   79

KATIA GRUBISIC   The End of Wolf Notes   80
                         The Rememberers   83

JOHN TERPSTRA   The Highway that became a Footpath   85

KIM GOLDBERG   Urban Getaway   87

MICHAEL deBEYER   Signal Flare Across the Vacant Shield 89
                         Cyclical Gesture: The Population
                              Forecast   89
                         Her Coming All Granite Upheaval   90

LISA ROBERTSON   Fourth Walk   91

• a leaf that looks like a mouth •

Ross Leckie	The Palm Walk	94
Erin Robinsong	Cog and Pine	96
	Turnery	98
	SEED : CEDE	99
	CEDE : SEED	100
Margaret Christakos	Wellington	101
A.Rawlings	STOP THEM, IF YOU, A PIECE	
	OF LAND, COULD YOU	109
	SUNDAY	110
	SHOCK, SPLINT	111
	THE GREAT LAKES	112
	SIGNS OF WHOM	114
	SIGNS OF ENGENDERMENT	116
	SIGNS OF ENDANGERMENT	116
	SIGNS OF EXTINCTION	116
Roger Nash	Sturgeon Petroglyph	117
	On Getting Yourself Conceived	118
Alison Calder & Jeanette Lynes	from *Ghost Works: Improvisations in Letters and Poems*	120
Kemeny Babineau	Global Weather Weil	125
	Question Marks	126
Christian Bök	A Virus from Outer Space	127
Notes on specific poems		*130*
Acknowledgments		*131*
Biographies		*134*

Introductions

The Astronauts
by Adam Dickinson

"Moonlight through high branches";
All poets say there's more to it
Than moonlight through high branches.

But me, what do I "know" about moonlight?
Sometimes I'm just under those branches, calling a lost cat,
Or in the house across the road, scribbling,
The moon's shining, that's moonlight for you,
And my neighbour's out in his car again, gunning the motor.
(Erin Mouré / Eirin Moure)[1]

THE MOON: pillar of poetry and science. The first lovers'
light, the first calendar. The driver of romantic tropes, and
shoreline ecosystems. The moon marks a curious intersection
of environments—both natural and cultural. Of this world
and outer space, it separates earthly wilderness from the wilds
beyond our most fundamental conceptions of mass, energy,
and time. Contested prize of the Cold War, it underscores
the degree to which natural phenomena can also become
cultural constructions, become environments of imaginative
exchange and conflict. The moon hangs in the sky as a beacon
of alternative thinking (full moon fever); however, it also

represents a cautionary example, a possible future of environ-
mental devastation. After all, we reserve the word "moonscape"
for places stripped and sterilized by the unscrupulous practices
of heavy industry, or for the aftermath of nuclear war. Nobody
wants to live on the moon unless they have to.

Synonymous with environmental destruction, Sudbury,
Ontario, has long been infamously associated with the moon.
NASA astronauts trained in locations around the city in the
early 1970s because of unique geological features. The Apollo
16 astronauts came to simulate moonwalks in lunar shatter
cones, which were believed to be similar to the impact crater
that formed the Sudbury Basin approximately 1.8 billion years
ago. Despite the purely scientific interest in Sudbury's geology,
it was popularly believed that the astronauts came because the
landscape resembled the barren surface of the moon. Indeed,
the denuded forests and contaminated soil caused by intensive
mining operations made it easy for this myth to take hold.

Despite its devastated moonscape reputation, Sudbury has
justifiably become famous for successful efforts at restoring
the ecological health of its sensitive and diverse ecosystems.
What is to be made of such transformations? How do we re-
imagine spaces in the act of restoring their diversity? How is the
capacity for re-imagination itself intrinsic to the ecology of such
transformative achievements? As Lawrence Buell has pointed
out, the environmental crisis is also a crisis of the imagination.[2]
We live our lives by metaphors, through discursive frames that
constrain the spectrum of significance. How do we change what
matters—ethically and materially?

There is, of course, a long tradition of imagined landscapes
in the history of pastoral poetry, where idealized rural
vistas become raw material for poetic reflection, for escapist
critiques of urban life, and for exaggerated amorous entreaties.

Contemporary writers, however, must wrestle with what it means, as Don McKay points out, "to come to grips with the practice of poetry in a time of environmental crisis."[3] It is no longer sufficient to stage singing contests among shepherds.[4] One way of marking the difference between the idealized environments of classical pastoral "nature poetry" and contemporary "ecological poetry," is to consider Juliana Spahr's distinction that "ecopoets" are concerned with "a poetics full of systematic analysis and critique that questions the divisions between nature and culture while also acknowledging that humans use up too much of the world."[5] Similarly, Jonathan Skinner, editor of the journal *ecopoetics*, argues, with emphasis on the etymology of *ecology* and *poiesis*, that ecopoetics is "house making," it is "a site for poetic attention and exchange" that does not subordinate the artistic environment of the poem to a separate referential environment of more urgent concern.[6] In other words, the ecopoem attends to the world-building (and world-effacing) capacities of language as well as to the natural and social worlds in which the poem is situated. We have used the term ecological poetry in this anthology with ecopoetics in mind. If anything, by emphasizing the two words, it is our intention to foreground the poetics of ecological dynamics and the ecology of rhetorical and formal poetic procedures. While we acknowledge the activist implications of a poetics of increased environmental consciousness, we also wish to underscore the ecology of different political possibilities in environmentally concerned writing. There are poems about pollution in this collection. Additionally, there are elegies, lyrical meditations, and pataphysical experiments that, by proposing imaginary solutions and exceptional methodologies, come at the question of environmental consciousness more obliquely and unconventionally.

11

Consequently, our aim in this anthology has been to bring together a diverse spectrum of current Canadian poets writing about the environment in formally and thematically varied ways. The innovative formal procedure of Queyras, for example, differs from the referential narrative style of Bartlett. Almon's moving anecdote about personal responsibility and endangered species stands out against Babineau's visual poem in the interrogative mode. Bondar's sprawling juxtaposition of the forests of Peru and Northern Ontario contrasts with the constrained precision of Bök's anagrammatic poem rendered as a protein. All of these works, however, provoke us to think about the way in which the environment is not simply a nonhuman wilderness that beckons us toward weekend escapes, but is in fact a composite, plural, interactive space of competing physical, social, and conceptual frames of signification.

An earlier Canadian environmentally focused anthology, Litteljohn and Pearce's *Marked by the Wild* (1973), emphasizes writing concerned with "wild nature" at the expense of urban environments; the editors defend their choice out of a conviction, following Northrop Frye, that the distinguishing element of Canadian literature is "the influence of the wild."[7] Of course, this raises questions about what defines the wild, or determines influence in the first place. To what degree do civically planned urban green spaces and water management strategies presuppose socially constructed apprehensions of the wild and the natural? Holmes's recent anthology of Canadian nature poems, *Open Wide a Wilderness* (2009), similarly focuses on "'wild' nature rather than 'domestic nature.'"[8] Though, it must be acknowledged, her decision comes not from willful neglect, but from a recognition of the necessity of thematic boundaries given the scope of the anthology's ambitious project (nature poems throughout Canadian history).

We have attempted to interpret the idea of environment broadly in this collection. The physical, social, and linguistic environments are all sites of inquiry. Some of these poems are explicitly activist in their political dimensions, some more implicitly so, raising ethical and epistemological questions about responsibility, technology, and community. The landscapes are often Canadian; nonetheless, in being Canadian, they are connected to other places, whether that is the multicultural complexity of urban spaces, or the imperial, multinational machinations of the tar sands and other industrial practices. In addition, Ireland, Peru, Arizona, and India appear as geographical intertexts, as deterritorializations of myth and local familiarity. Despite the fact that a number of these poems are rooted in quintessentially Canadian geography, we make no claims for a distinctly national ecological poetics. The concerns and practices of these poets are as varied as the Canadas that do and do not appear in their works.

The book is divided into three sections, which, depending on your perspective, both broaden and narrow the environmental focus. On the one hand, the three sections can be seen as a movement from specific natural environments, to more amorphous social and built environments, to, finally, larger more abstract fields of communication and environments of signification. On the other hand, the three sections can be seen as a movement toward increasingly specific frameworks of concern: from the referential world of objects, places, and animals, to the localized and compressed world of cities and economies, to, finally, the world of signs in the constrained fields of linguistic association. This expanding or contracting focus enacts the multiple and irreducible dynamics at work in these poems and in ecological systems more generally. Of course, it goes without saying that these sections are not meant to imply a rigid formal or thematic taxonomy. Rather, poems may often fit into more than one section. Take Robertson's "Fourth Walk," for example. As a site-specific work, it could fit easily into the first section with its emphasis on localities and places; however, with its exploration of signifying surfaces in the ruined factories of a Vancouver industrial district, Robertson's piece could also fit into the third section with its more explicit concern for the semiotics of reading and writing environments. The three sections of the anthology are meant to be perspectives rather than prescriptions.

The first section, "a triumph of tubers," collects poems overtly engaged with specific landscapes, objects, or phenomena. There is often in these poems direct exploration of environmental localities and situations, or, more generally speaking, the referential world. Poems in this section include Harris's spiritual meditations on a river, Pierson's visceral investigations of shrinking glaciers, Hoogland's metaphorical depictions of a boy walking on snow and reckoning with evolutionary history, Ruffo's and Chénier's childhood recollections of Sudbury and Falconbridge precipitated by encounters with pollution, and McKay's site-specific work about the Muskwa-Kechika wilderness area in Northern British Columbia.

The second section, "pristine modernity, the dream," collects poems more actively concerned with the social and built environment. In this section, cities, myths, traffic, and industrial projects become sites of inquiry into the economic and social consequences of different relations with and attitudes towards the environment. Many of these poems are concerned with the way in which consumer capitalism and the "dream of modernity" become environments themselves that frame the way in which people interpret and interact with the world around them. Terpstra explores the social and natural history at the site of a highway expansion in Hamilton; Wong investigates the complex interactions between race, economics, and technology; Goldberg observes the rhizomatic lines of flight in a city "shepherding its soundless parts, obedient as a shorn herd of silicon chips or a flock of rebar encased in blind faith"; Rowley presents a call to action against the transnational military-industrial interests driving the development of the tar sands in her ironic appeal to "wade in the tailing ponds" and enjoy the "smell of crude oil / in the morning"; deBeyer combines discourses of geometry, psychoanalysis, and the science of human settlements in his pataphysical excavation of the natural laws of Ayr, Ontario.

The third section of the anthology, "a leaf that looks like a mouth," collects poems directly engaged with questions of significance and signification in the context of reading and writing the environment. In works by Christakos, Robinsong, Calder and Lynes, for example, syllables, homonyms, and homolinguistic translations become environments in which the materiality of reference circulates, and language becomes a field of ecological relations; Leckie exhorts us to read (and read like) palm trees; a.rawlings explores the subtle semiotic interplay between signs of engenderment, endangerment, and extinction. The poems in this section remind us to think not simply of the biosphere, but also of the semiosphere, of the world of signification in which we live.[9] It is difficult to care about things we do not see, or that do not signify for us. Clearly, one of the imperatives of environmental activism must be to broaden fields of signification, expand horizons of significance so that creatures, places, and biodiversity matter in increasingly urgent ways.

The last poem in the third section, Christian Bök's "A Virus from Outer Space," is an especially appropriate work with which to close the anthology in part because it recalls Sudbury's geological connections with asteroids and outer space. Moreover, the becoming-protein of the poem also expands both conceptually and physically the notion of what constitutes an ecological poem. What are the limits to an environment? Where do humans end and viruses or misbehaving proteins begin? Perhaps language really did come from outer space; look how much we have learned from the moon. Bök's forthcoming *The Xenotext Experiment* pushes some of these questions even further by encoding a poem into the genetic material of a bacterium. This experiment exposes provocatively how we not only write the world around us, but also how the world re-writes our writing, as subsequent expressions of the affected genes within the bacterium are expected to manufacture new benign proteins that will alter the original poem.[10] We must rethink reified distinctions between culture and nature, between human and nonhuman, between science and poetry. The poems in this collection do precisely this in diverse and multifaceted ways.

Originally, this was going to be a book about Sudbury. While the thematic focus for the anthology has broadened, Sudbury nonetheless remains as a literal and figurative vein running through and between many of these poems. As astronauts, you are invited to explore the entropies and topographies of this terrain.

Notes

[1] Erin Mouré, *Sheep's Vigil by a Fervent Person: A Transelation of Alberto Caeiro / Fernando Pessoa's O Guardador de Rebanhos* (Toronto: Anansi Press, 2001) 91.

[2] Lawrence Buell, *The Environmental Imagination: Thoreau, Nature Writing, and the Formation of American Culture* (Cambridge, MA, London: Harvard University Press, 1995) 2.

[3] Don McKay, *Vis à Vis: Fieldnotes on Poetry and Wilderness* (Wolfville, NS: Gaspereau Press, 2001) 9.

[4] It is important to point out that a number of contemporary Canadian poets have re-imagined the pastoral genre in ways open to ecologies of natural and social history. See, for example, Lisa Robertson's *XEclogue* and *Occasional Work and Seven Walks from the Office for Soft Architecture*, as well as Erin Mouré's *Sheep's Vigil by a Fervent Person*.

[5] Juliana Spahr, *things of each possible relation hashing against one another* (Newfield, NY: Palm Press, 2003) 29.

[6] Jonathan Skinner, "Statement for 'New Nature Writing' Panel at 2005 AWP (Vancouver)," *ecopoetics* 4/5 (2004-2005): 127-128.

[7] Bruce Litteljohn and Jon Pearce, eds., *Marked by the Wild: An anthology of literature shaped by the Canadian wilderness* (Toronto: McClelland and Stewart, 1973) 11.

[8] Nancy Holmes, ed., *Open Wide a Wilderness: Canadian*

Nature Poems (Waterloo: Wilfrid Laurier University Press, 2009) xv.

[9] The term "semiosphere" is borrowed from biosemiotics, in particular the writings of Jesper Hoffmeyer who defines the semiosphere as "a sphere just like the atmosphere, the hydrosphere, and the biosphere. It penetrates to every corner of these other spheres, incorporating all forms of communication: sounds, smells, movements, colors, shapes, electrical fields, thermal radiation, waves of all kinds, chemical signals, touching, and so on. In short, signs of life" (vii). Jesper Hoffmeyer, *Signs of Meaning in the Universe*, trans. Barbara J. Haveland (Bloomington and Indianapolis: Indiana University Press, 1996).

[10] See: Christian Bök, "The Xenotext Experiment," *SCRIPTed* 5:2 (2008): 227-331.

Gap Dynamics
by Madhur Anand

I look down
in the dead waters
of Sudbury and
I think of Flaubert
    (Miriam Waddington)[1]

ON APRIL 14, 2009, the first-ever historical anthology of Canadian nature poems was launched in Guelph, Ontario. The volume's editor, Nancy Holmes, remarked that what we need now is an anthology of new nature poems. We feel *Regreen* answers that need, but not in any premeditated manner. Unfilled niches in the poetic world are not leftover space, but new space created in the understory of towering legacies. In the gaps caused by small disturbances to forests, diversity regenerates and perpetuates itself, just as poets, like seedlings in forests, "burst out, to find new openings, new windows" (Robyn Sarah). As Don McKay puts it, "death is made up entirely of ecological niches-to-be." Gaps of different sizes support different communities. The science of ecology hypothesizes that diversity thrives most where there are moderate levels of disturbance; likewise, one may expect that an anthology of poems about ecological disturbance should itself be quite diverse. For this reason, we have not wanted to focus solely on environmental devastation, which reduces the scope of diversity. We want to explore the more subtle effects of disturbance and contemplate a world that has not been destroyed beyond recovery.

The idea for this anthology began to germinate some time between 2000 and 2006. I was living in Sudbury and studying its unique ecology, a history of utter devastation and inspirational restoration. During this same period I began to take poetry more seriously, publishing my first poems and thinking about theoretical links between poetry and my research in ecological modeling. Questions occurred to me for which a traditional scientific approach just did not seem to be sufficient: why restore, what to restore, where was the line dividing tradition and novelty or conservation and preservation, and what was the role of chance and adaptation? What was to be made of such transformations? How do we re-imagine spaces in the act of restoring their diversity? In what manner are figurative and physical relationships with place altered through restoration and reclamation processes?

But let's start with the word "green." Think of leaves—the thousands of blades that make up summer lawns, the cotyledons and bright fiddleheads that poke through the hard brown ground in spring, the space-filling, shadow-creating summer canopy of maple, birch or poplar. I visualize Rhea Tregebov's "trees and sky" somewhere on the road between Toronto and Sudbury in May; Maureen Scott Harris's "tangle of small willows crowding / the bank, leaning over their reflections...." Green is the colour of the growing season; the word itself is etymologically related to the Old English word for "grow." But 'regreen' is a neologism. It refers to the process by which the colour green (or what it represents) is returned to its proper place. The loss of green implies death and decay: "there are ideas...you may not like" (Sina Queyras); there are other colours, such as rust (around the neck of a heron in Karen Houle's poem) or just plain black (Rhonda Collis's "black rocks, black lungs"). At some point, as Ruth Roach Pierson finds, there is nothing to contemplate but white and "ablation", a word referring at once to the removal of disease and the melting glaciers. One meaning moves us in a clear direction towards former health while the other points simply towards barrenness, and a fresh start. Through the insight of poets like Armand Ruffo we see that regreening requires "a new kind of thinking / that was actually old." Brian Bartlett envisions a lunar landscape "where centuries / pass before anyone picks apart a box / and finds a few poems from our time, / ...the island...struggling back to the tempests / and the snowfalls, to photosynthesis and moulds...." The poems themselves lying dormant, like seeds full of potential.

The transnational mining corporation Inco (now the Brazilian-owned Vale Inco) has spent millions of dollars to "regreen" the denuded landscape surrounding Sudbury—a breathtaking recovery for which Sudbury has won numerous awards, but somehow has not yet shaken the city from its polluted reputation. We can thus, at another level, think of regreen as refund, a paying back of ecological debt, and we have a long way to go. Erin Robinsong examines the entangled link between ecology and economy in a way that defies simple causal relationships. But even despite our best efforts to "cede the best," she finds that "the math makes no sense." Walking around in a post-industrial site, Lisa Robertson notices "the economies that could not appear in money..." and finds the world "leaning and budding and scraping, as if it too was subjected to strange rules never made explicit." These and other poems bring forth new ideas about the difficulty of quantifying

21

a process that is so entwined with our senses and beliefs—the complex humanistic relationship to the natural world. Rita Wong describes a "green trust" in which "the next shift may be the biggest one yet, the union of the living, from mosquito to manatee to mom."

Re-membering

Nothing in the open systems of nature can be repeated: the irreversibility of time persists, despite nostalgia and any attempt to record the past in order to reproduce it. But our desire to turn back time continues nontheless. Jan Conn makes the plea: "Couldn't we begin again / with a bed of straw?" Even the word "relive" means to experience something again, often as a result of just thinking about it. It occurs for the most part in the human mind, which cannot perfectly recreate history:

> Remembering is not the re-excitation of innumerable fixed, lifeless, and fragmentary traces. It is an imaginative reconstruction, or construction, built out of the relation of our attitude towards a whole active mass of organized past reactions or experience, and to a little outstanding detail which commonly appears in image or in language form. It is thus hardly ever really exact, even in the most rudimentary cases of rote recapitulation, and it is not at all important that it should be so.[2]

Restoration ecology is the science that puts into practice the process of remembering. It is a kind of reinvention of ecological systems through an imaginative remembering that allows for the simultaneous existence of a diversity of ecological assemblages, many of our own making. Restoration, like remembering itself, is not a passive process, but an active one in which we construct new realities. Mari-Lou Rowley writes of the necessity of imagining a future based on the past but acknowledges its inherent difficulty. Her very use of language reflects this: "make me perfect, past / tense and release, past / learning from mistakes / past-present, future-perfect / oh perfector of defects." Katia Grubisic advises us that "Memory is not the same as come back; / it is not the same as letting go."

Most of the healing in the Sudbury landscape has involved the seeding of non-native plants and the planting of native and non-native trees. Why? Because these were believed to be the only plant species capable of quickly (and economically) covering the barren hills. Some have wondered about the species composition (or lack thereof) of Sudbury's regreened landscape. At some level, the dozens of plant species that make up a native Canadian forest become mere outlines of themselves. Regreen becomes the ecological equivalent of applying a broad stroke of green paint across the landscape. But what about the thousands of shades and forms that green actually represents? My own scientific research in the area attempts to assess the success, the long-term fate of these novel ecosystems: How can they be rendered sustainable? How to adapt regreening processes in light of our increasing knowledge about restoration ecology? The idea is to bring the ecosystems back to a point where they can begin to 're-member' themselves—something akin to Michael deBeyer's "unkempt pathway...like lying down in humus, recomposition crowding over your limbs."

The classical theory of natural succession imposes a certain sequence on the appearance of assemblages on forest landscapes: lichens and mosses, to grasses and herbs, to a "climax" (stable-state) of shrubs and trees. As such, it is not unreasonable to expect regreening or reforestation to follow a similar process.

The ordering of the poems in this book suggests one possible sequence which we felt might help guide the reader. However, just as the old ecological ideas about succession as a process that moves predictably towards a "climax" state remains challenged by considerations of spatial and temporal scales of observation and disturbance, the poems here may be read in any order the reader chooses to fit his or her relationship to the book.

Restoration ecology ultimately comes down to finding the answer to simple questions: what to plant, and how and where to plant it. Literally, re-membering. But there is much debate among ecologists about what exactly we are trying to do, which species should be used, what should be recaptured. Ecologists realize that it is not possible to reinstate ecosystems exactly the way they were (that is, to return all species to formerly observed places and proportions), but rather the goal is to improve things like ecosystem "function" (productivity, stability and resilience). However, it is often the case that those responsible for restoration are not ecologists, but rather people who wish to restore that which is immediately appreciable, such as aesthetic beauty. Indeed, the staying power of nostalgia is such that it is very difficult to convince some individuals that different assemblages of species can have the same function. Everyone is fearful of non-native species because some of them can become invasive and create havoc, like out-competing native species and reducing overall diversity. Very recently, a paper published in the scientific journal *Ecological Restoration* called for 'a new kind of language' to move the emphasis from the dominantly technical one, to one in which aesthetic, functional and social values of restoration become integrated. This book is another kind of attempt to broaden views on the role of language itself in helping to solve the environmental crisis.

Don McKay writes that the concept of wilderness is "so overwritten it should probably be granted a reprieve from definition, maybe even a lengthy sabbatical from speech." What is it about wilderness that makes us think we can destroy it, immediately regret we did, and then spend our lifetimes trying to recapture it? In some of my field sites, I have come across hundreds of tiny jack pine seedlings evenly spaced in neat rows on blackened rock. These have been planted by citizens desperate to see the pine forests come back quicker than on their own or by the City's regreening plan, which takes care of some hillsides before others. People seem to forget the fact that jack pines need fire to regenerate and before that a layer of soil held in place by various understory species to put down roots. A pine is a pine is a pine. It does not seem to matter that the Great Lakes-St. Lawrence forest, characterized mainly by white and red pine, is what dominated the Sudbury landscape before the industrial damage. I have actually pulled out some of the planted jack pine seedlings, knowing they have no chance of survival.

I am, perhaps, in the right place for this kind of almost luxurious investigation: "A university is an oasis," claims Ross Leckie, contemplating the planted palm trees on the campus of the University of Arizona in the middle of the Sonoran desert. He captures the feeling of displaced individuals: "I need the encouragement of trees / that say this is a kind of boulevard / pointed toward an anonymous building / with black windows;" and later "the stacks are open, though it's better if you don't know / the word stacks. It's too depressing." Monique Chénier takes the almost opposite view, invoking the exotic in the domestic task of gathering fruit from wild native species that need no reintroduction, the ones which persist in ecological memory: "The sand dunes where we pick are / As I imagine a

25

desert would be / Soft and smelling of blueberries / The tang of invisible pine needles sharpening the air." But unlike the oasis of Leckie, she describes her surrounding as "an almost barren land that can be reached by car."

Our ability to regreen and indeed our collective definition of the term, depends upon our ability to understand evolutionary pathways, spatial ecologies, imagined realities and complex causal relationships in which our own human identity is affected by our relationship to the environment. Several poems in the volume demonstrate this kind of understanding. In a.rawlings's series of "Signs" poems, we are presented with the fragmented connections that often exist between an early phase of ecological awareness ("Signs of Whom") through a downward path towards extinction. These self-conscious recordings of loss express simultaneously the process by which language itself can become degraded. Margaret Christakos's "six elongated stanzas as if crazed by nostalgia" finds a world of refuge in the most imperfect of places, a small street called Wellington Heights: "I agree, the hill is an irk of a hill and needs / leaving, repaving, the flattening crush of loaded sky." These kinds of imaginative refugia are just as important as any real refugia, such as patches of relatively undisturbed forest that have recently been discovered close to historic smelters and which are seen as important points of nucleation for recovery. Alanna F. Bondar is cautious about the power of the human hand in reshaping landscapes and global ecological change. She wants "to stumble into the caverns of fire ants, their tiny round bodies are too perfect, a shape built for joining, for carrying tiny green leaves on my back, out of the jungle and into the forests of Northern Ontario. But something lesser in me makes me want to kill them before they grow mouths/ hands that say something in a language I do not understand."

Cornelia Hoogland expresses the resilience of both scientific and poetic approaches to understanding ecology in the "deepest understanding...metaphor."

During a recent visit to Science North in Sudbury, I witnessed an eight-year-old girl scream at the sight of a live green frog behind glass walls. A strange juxtaposition of the "greenhorn" and the "green-eyed monster" (Olive Senior). Or is this already a kind of premature fossilization, which, as Roger Nash puts it, occurs when a species moves "successfully through putrid waters into pristine nowhere"? Or Bert Almon's specimen in the glass bell, where the language of fossilization itself becomes guilty of self-conscious possession: "I have, I have..."? Alison Calder and Jeannette Lynes struggle with a similar sense of loss in their "imprint" poems: "The leaf imprint wouldn't photograph...Now I must rely on memory, on resemblances: a leaf that looks like a mouth." At several points the musing moves beyond human images towards God and the Universe. But Jane Munro warns us that "suckled by gods, even an ant could grow / as galaxies grow—demonic." On contemplating the demise of a city, Kim Goldberg conjectures that "the City may have reformulated itself into white dwarfs and red giants in the winter skies, which astrophysicists now know are actually reflections of glistening fish guts wrapped tight as shrunken cowhide at the centre of the earth." From his "privileged" place on the Niagara Escarpment, John Terpstra's imagines a "new city" that "came down out of heaven." Kemeny Babineau suggests that "either way we'll get it all / and have a hand, thus, in re creation / but more like a god gone wrong: / hand snapped in the weather wheel...." Christian Bök, following William Burroughs, claims that "language is a virus from outer space" and has ventured upon a completely novel experiment: to infect DNA, the language of life itself, with poetry.

In August 2007 I wrote to Laurence Steven at Your Scrivener Press with the idea to edit a book of new poems about 'restoration ecology'. The goal was to seek submissions (aiming at unpublished work or very recently published work) which would best respond to our call within the limits of a relatively small volume. It seemed fitting that a Sudbury publisher take on a book inspired by Sudbury's landscapes. The poems here, however, we expect to travel far beyond Sudbury, far beyond inspiration.

Notes

[1] Miriam Waddington, "Dead Lakes," *Open Wide a Wilderness: Canadian Nature Poems*. Ed. Nancy Holmes (Waterloo: Wilfrid Laurier University Press, 2009) 177-178.

[2] F.C. Bartlett, *Remembering* (Cambridge, England: Cambridge University Press, 1932) 213.

"a triumph of tubers"

Rhea Tregebov

ELEGY FOR THE WILD

"Trees and sky," the woman behind me says, "just trees and sky."
On the bus north to Sudbury the land fills me up.
I think we think we're more important than we are.
Three rows back a kid coos
like a pigeon, ready for sleep,
a dream of trees.
Beautiful wild country.
Now the boy's a soft, mournful siren.
He's tired, he's so tired and the bus
is a rough cradle. It's May,
and snow still stands in the deepest shade,
in the place where it's always winter.
I want to keep looking.
I want to keep looking till I'm done.
Country. Beautiful country. Beautiful wild country.

Maureen Scott Harris

BE THE RIVER

Be the river then, straight or crooked,
its hidden energy pulling it ever down
at a speed that's barely visible. Be
its red clay trough, be the way it wears
its own being-in-motion into place there,
the polished and runnelled banks which
curve and hold, be both flow and bank
and then the rising above. Be the air above
which pushes against its surface smoothing
or ruffling, snatching for something.
Be the tangle of small willows crowding
the bank, leaning over their reflections,
growing dizzy watching the clouds drift
among the fish beneath them. Be willows
and be too the stones in the gravel bank
whose slight movements mirror the way
water meets air, who bask in weather
and are patient. Be the silt washing in
from the rain, and the muskrat swirling
at the bank, be the splash and trickle of
sounds without identity, half-formed words
surfacing, do you hear? Be the swallows
who skim along the water's surface twisting
their narrow wings to rise and dart and
dip down again. Be all these and more,
whatever falls into the water and through
its skin to find the robust and hidden depths,
tumbling towards its wide mouth, singing.

31

Bert Almon

A Duty of Care

"The beast of the field shall honour me,
the dragons and the owls:
because I give waters in the wilderness,
and rivers in the desert."—Isaiah 43:20

Michael pulled over on the road
between Cork and Dunmanway
to show me where a wild swan
once flew into the power lines
and burst into flames.
He thought he should bury it
and carried it to his car.
How heavy the smoldering body was,
and the current had blown a hole in it.
The path from the fallen swan
to his light switch in Drinagh
was traceable in theory,
Michael thought.
The law of damages
has an inexhaustible phrase,
"to owe a duty of care."

Michael raises barn owls
in tree boxes. The species
grows more and more uncommon.
This morning in Ballydehob
we stood at an Antiques window
where a Wildlife Conservancy poster

showed a barn owl. The caption read,
"Have You Seen This Bird?"
"Yes, I have," Michael said,
pointing to a glass bell
in the same window, holding a specimen
whose only visible flaw was death.
He kept repeating the question
and its answer, "Yes, I have, I have."

Cornelia Hoogland

THE SCIENCE (AND POETRY) OF WHAT'S HARD-WIRED

The boy's walking on snow, on snow piled up 3 or 4 inches
beside the cleared sidewalk which is where he should be
    walking
yells the daycare worker from the head of the rope
all the daycare children clutch at intervals like a zigzag
snake—intermittent flashes
of yellow, a kind of theatrical performance—
except it's a safety device, nothing magical about it, *ye listenin'*
get on the sidewalk—what do you think a sidewalk's for?
She might have added what do you think the custodian
    cleared the snow for,
or the construction worker poured the cement for,
or the architect added the sidewalk around the building for.

That's when the Sturgeon River—where the boy in my
    mind lives—
picks up beside deer trails he walks on.
Fir needles, dirt, vegetation—and this past fall—
bear scat and rotting fish making what we call soil
beneath his boots. He can feel it. Springy, supplying reason
he's here on earth. Shaping the roots
of his deepest understanding, his metaphor.

He watches the Pike after day disintegrate,
leak their nutrients into the soil
that furnish the cedars, the White Pine. He can tell you
how it works: that wolves eat only the heads of fish
they carry back to their dens. Whole forests get fertilized
    this way.

But he's back at daycare with his evolutionary desire
to test himself
against the elements: the way
snow doesn't seem it should—but does—hold him;
the crunching sound he'll need in grade 8 for the poetry
    assignment;
the way his foot prints an angle,
a whole series of angles; mathematical tricks

of balance.

THE STORY OF ART

How it begins
with a three-year-old girl,
an itchy palm,
and *where are my flip-flops*
yelled at top volume.

The garden as she left it,
sleeping. Squash flowers
like rumpled Kleenex.

Her eyes see what her hand wants.
Bricks. Fifteen or so
line the herb garden
beside the shed.
Her fingers barely
span the width of the brick
she lifts—*lid off a pan*
and *O!* hundreds of thousands of
crickets and pill bugs scuttle for cover.

It's what she makes happen.
The world yelling back.

Alanna F. Bondar

WHAT IN THE TALL TREES? STACKS MADE FOR UNDOING
& LEAVES THE SHAPE OF REACHING
(from *there are many ways to die while travelling in peru*)

I take the path without rails on the backside edge of a Quechuan guide whose teeth chew through the forest, teach me how to taste leaves the size of wishes against unwanted fetuses. I spit it out, take the stems of coca to back home and in rounded crystal, cities linked by train/ the highway, Sudbury to the Sault. At an early age I hesitated to lick the taste of Sudbury air, rocks rolling the giant monkey frog into hunting these clouds with fists. I thought Sudbury was Hell and hoped my mother would choose Siberia instead. Each time passing colourless stubble/ low-lying human shuffles/ and picking the blue dots of purgatory like worm collectors/ mining helmets searching the ground for signs of viable earth. Even now, the curse remains emanating from the centre of an ancient crater, two hundred and ten kilometers of misery/ every time I go, I come back alone.

In the Amazonian jungle, blue dot pickers scatter unstuck in the past—ants scavenging remnants/ post apocalyptic sanitization. They become as before now, something to be feared/ how their bites from fire go down/ first stick of wood, first flame, first love and lost—after two weeks without phone calls, she has no words for him when they chance meet in the grocery store.// How the fourth sounds like a train whistle, black and white braces against the tracks, path through the snow and straight line home one way to the edge of purgatory. How the fourth looks like a television show where people appear in patterns. At first, in twos, visual pairings and then transcribed into textual twos, looking nothing alike but carrying the same book, having the same name, speaking the small inaudible language.// I could never become Sudbury, never the top of my father's head brush-cut and angry, the impulse to grow us straight into tall trees without voices for the speaking to skies and clouds and wings. In my coma I wonder what they are reading to me; someday I will brush past Salad Fingers, fit glass slippers of the forest, and be someone else's Honey Barbara.

As I spit it out, the Quechuan forest emerges inhabited by people I have never known—not in books or dreams or memories. The mother adds protein to our *cheecha* drink the mashing of cassava and her own spit to ferment/ she squirts breast milk into the bowl. We drink it lip to lip, mouth to mouth, strangers to the metal swamp. Sandy catches it too far on his beard before we can stop it/ film to slow. Cut. And words long/ train whistles between crossings. He swings it across his shadow, hits his wife between the letters, n and o/ catches her in the eye/ the space between. Edge of the metal bowl passed between us marks the hesitation, labels the spit of a fear worse than what's that/ bottom of the bog. Variation on the theme, fingers slip a note and railroad tracks melt boards in the afternoon sun, snow in the cervices. I flatten a penny on the track but it doesn't work without the train. Goldberg a bird of open jazz around the note.

And the leaf-cutters move silently, single handedly in a line; they pretend not to remember all they have forgotten. Each ant fights not to be first/ responsibility of revolution as high as uncle mike's folded and stacked grocery bags in the basement and jungle necklaces of brown wood and flat green heads. Mirrors, pianos, sofas, windows, rolled carpets, chairs and wardrobes, their backs clinging the movement of each piece moved, a line hugs the branch and drop. Theirs cling without breaking/ they know how to look from a bird's eye view but choose not to. Somewhere paper mache is taking a bite out of mine and in its mouth the taste of paste/ postage stamps, stamps reading the backs of hands and tasting the green edge of spit. The mouth a funny place to travel.

There are tears in the hems of the tallest trees fragmented by a *doppleganger* thousands of kilometers away. Inco 1972 Superstack three hundred and eighty metres into the abject/ air from the continuity of leaf-cutters who move across the litres, step by step, putting tiny stitches into print. Soon we will not forgot our connections over coffee, the dissolving shape conversations take when they sketch nothing of the ant itself. Their collections guard caravans to be unrolled, laid on top of one another—maps on maps with tissue taking what's underneath the hand and lifting it, layer by layer, until the whole planet formed by paper mache begins to grow leaves and grass, and paint pink over tar-stained granite. Each stitch a print stretching itself—one by one—to pages meant for turning, black markings and the ants.

I want to stumble into the caverns of fire ants, their tiny round bodies are too perfect; a shape built for joining, for carrying tiny green leaves on my back—out of the jungle and into the forests of Northern Ontario. But something lesser in me makes me want to kill them before they grow mouths/ hands that say something in a language I do not understand. I pass the *cheecha* back to the mother, the one holding a small child who pees down the side of her body, drizzles the ends of a tiny bladder onto her legs. This mother has no hesitation in not noticing. Like pudicity, she holds her breast with the other hand, flicks an ant off the edge of the bowl, the others Halkans in the Tantalus Field.// Cutting the fold, what's left after the torn edges of kapok trees have been scattered above by the Superstack, all five hundred and sixty-two pieces of them blue? A *palma real*, simulacrum of the telephone pole beside it, eighteen metres high. And cloud-maker, super-high chimney, still mirror-mirroring a jungle giant. For us to make it undone is to really/ really/ really want the sky.

Monique Chénier

FALCONBRIDGE 1964-1975

It exists in a series of wheres
Stationary moments of
Walking jumping and scraping a knee against pavement
In one Grandma stands just inside the coolness of the garage
Amongst smells of grey paint and clean clothes
She spits to ease the pain

In another she bends over a low bush
While my grandfather is busy with pails further away
A menthol cigarette hanging from his lips
The sand dunes where we pick are
As I imagine a desert would be
Soft and smelling of blueberries
The tang of invisible pine needles sharpening the air
An almost barren land that can be reached by car

In town the smell of sulfur rises
From summer heat on melted rocks
The black and copper swirls that line the road and train
    tracks
Are not beautiful but their iridescence
Holds my eye
Until I want to touch one and keep it hidden
Everything has a slightly yellow look here
As though the west sun must slant down
Through smoky clouds and burn its way through

Inside the backyard fence behind the clean garage

Of my grandparents' home
The light is different under the shade of two apple trees
Their garden of raspberries
Red and black currants
Carrots peas yellow and green beans
A compost heap where nothing is wasted—
A place where nothing is lost—
Is a lush contrast to the parched land that lies beyond
Even manure smells good here as it is worked
Through pea pods and expired plants

And then behind their home
A different kind of desert stretches flat out
Toward the stable and the tracks
Its sand resembles the molten rock now crushed to coarse
    meal
Not pleasant to walk on but leading to a secret place
Outside the oasis of their yard and tucked against its back
    fence
A cave of scrub perfect for children
Seeking refuge from the heat of make believe
And dying of thirst

To me this town was perfect
Because of who was there
Because of every scrap of cellophane or foil that was kept
Or reused
Because of the quarter jar that took a year to save
Because everything they had was loved and became lovely

Jan Conn

Monsoon, Early June

The lemon-yellow building with detachable steeple
cools me down in milliseconds.

My triangular hand-made hat-box and I zoom toward it
on a dragon fly, there's fresh snow on the ridge

and a caribou head with antlers as paperweights
in the corner office of some city tower—

Did I say an abbreviated version of a Buddhist chant,
a single inhalation with the one good lung left

after sandpaper was aggressively applied?
Monsoon, early June, I'm up to my neck in it.

Tipsy rectangle plunks itself down casually
beside haute chartreuse and a volcano

erupts on the ocean floor, the ash blending just so
with the de-accelerating mid-Atlantic current.

My soul shrunken to the size of a minnow
gasps for water, flops on the eroded bank

of a Pliocene river—Couldn't we begin again
with a bed of straw? Open the coal-black door

beneath the overhang, hold one finger
under the rusted hot-water tap, run for cover

inside the twice-repaired admiral's jacket.

43

ANIMATED PLANTS

Strolling across cerulean snow in the intermediate realm

    animated plants above ground, and below
a triumph of tubers, roots, vegetative stuffing

        Giant stick insects take their places among the conifers

The narcotic wind keeps us from feeling any loss too deeply

our reflections trapped in ever-widening gaps between panes
    no longer recognizable as self

Something pink occurs, bareheaded and bare backed

    A child is jammed into the back seat between two
        slabs of beef, a rodeo taking place in the next town

No water in the aquifer

    A solitary bee
        heads straight as an arrow to a redbud on a hilltop

Do you have a point of view? Harmless and aimless,
    sexual fantasy's voluptuousness disappointing in the flesh

    —she's inconsolable and burying corpses
                with the gravedigger's son

Here in the east, larkspurs stir and the lost traveller
    finds his way in the hailstorm, having left windows open

in every previous town

Ruth Roach Pierson

A SCREE OF CRYSTALLINE BLISTERS
    (After Elaine Whittaker's art installation "Ablation")

shards of home-grown salt

      surgically

   excised and placed

       in precariously hung

Petri dishes

   their shadows' glimmer

      Devon

    Ross

a harbinger

   Penny

 Ayles

of glaciers' accelerating shrinkage

  Melville

   Meighan

an adumbration of ice fields'

   Agassiz

Larsen B.

break-up into ice-pan bric-à-brac

Ward Hunt

Filchner-Ronne

White

for the scientist explorers

white

for ablation   the totality of erosion

white

purged of blue

white for oblivion

and the oblivious

white for salt and salt

for the coming dessication

for the salt crystals left

at the edge of receding seas

the salt that encrusts

the lips of the thirsty

46

Heat wave

a misnomer for this sodden hogwash, wa-
sabi hot, smothering the city—June, July,
August—no end in sight. Waves, after all,

abate—like those heard on cool
Phinney Bay summer nights, stars
falling through a Van Gogh sky to the slap,
slurp, slap of passing craft. Now,

in this land-locked urban space, the forecast "un-
abated" chafes. A straw that breaks—

that's what I crave. Also wane and ebb,
finitude: the day lily's swift
wilt, stars dying before we see their light.

That window's double-glazed pane,
this rock—a slow shattering.

Brian Bartlett

LEAVING THE ISLAND

Leprous paint flakes off a lighthouse
   whose last glow has faded to sparkless nothing.
     No glass lingers in the windows
of the long-buried keeper's house, red roof-tiles
   flung far, leaving pale patches where the many rains
     seep through. Footpaths have disappeared more fully
than fossils and cutlery. The island is going back
   to the northeasterlies, the south-
     westerlies, to the basalt and mica and granite.

The man who tended the light grew a garden
   since dissolved like a pill in water. Yarrow rises
through the gaps between separating slats
   of a landed boat, lime-green lichen streaking it,
     the only passengers wind-catapulted rocks
that find no rower to take them anywhere.
   The island is going back to the arctic terns
     riding the winds in quick, unwritten patterns,
to the nesting cormorants lifting their flexible necks
   like nude eccentric trees. All metal has rusted,
     all paper sun-yellowed, dampened and dried
thousands of times. A dusky guillemot chick
   tries out its first steps, pecks at a dead gannet's flesh
     and peeps, the closest human ear
miles away: a man and his daughter in a dory,
   Annie watching TV on a laptop with ear-phones
     (Californian school girl hides her identity
as famous pop-star) while her father adjusts a net.

May this be like a lunar surface where centuries
    pass before anybody picks apart a box
      and finds a few poems from our time,
photos of geniuses, and headlines of Word War III
    ending. Though pockets of froth among rocks
      turn out to be bits of Styrofoam—
though a strip of water shining like cellophane
    is cellophane, and a beer can flung from the dory
      starts its long jagged course to this shore—
the island is going back to the tempests
    and the snowfalls, to photosynthesis and moulds,
      to the endless rubbing of water on immigrant glass.

Robyn Sarah

AS A STORM-LOPPED TREE

As a storm-lopped tree corrects its shape
over a few green seasons, so time
closes around the hole in itself
left by the terrible event.

(in the quiet room suddenly the ice
in your glass hisses and cracks—)

So years have carried you, far beyond
the site of your old derailment,
the place where once you caused
harm to yourself and others;
it is behind you now,
and the damage, behind us all.

The chain belt of time
runs around and around.
Moon walks where it wants to,
like cats in high places.
Sun gilds the buildings...

And moments of animal well-being
may be all that's left us, may well be.

To be grateful for neutral days.

To snip a strip of char
from a blackened wick, then watch
how the lamp comes alive again.

FOR LIGHT

Things are, that are. So, to learn is to learn not to play the philosopher; not to say that what is not to be, is not meant to be, is for the best. Let it be enough that doors close.

Lately I have been thinking that there must be two ways to leave this world; one, by a continual opening up, the other by a continual closing. Most of us take the latter route, shutting off our accesses as we are burned by them, the doors of curiosity, of chance, of imagining, sealed off one by one, till little by little the being closes in on itself, shuts itself into the dark. When no more light can get in, when there is no more looking, that is the end. Rare are the ones who go the other way—who keep the doors open, who are always punching out new holes, new openings, till they are all window, and invaded totally by light they meld with it, they become light themselves.

Of course I know that it is not so simple. But I know that as I get older, my life becomes more and more a struggle against the impulse to shut doors, a struggle to keep alive the counter-impulse, to burst out, to find new openings, new windows. Windows, that are for looking and for light.

GATE

A pause to pull socks up.

It seems the time has come
to check your raggedy sadnesses
at the gate,
and take your place in line again
for the roulette of days.

Time to turn your back on
that other one, your nemesis,
a face that looks backward and weeps
while the feet walk blind
into the future;
time to drop hands with that one.

You have come into a place
of unbleached reckoning.
It is like
an empty dress,
wind filling an empty dress
hung out to air,
revolving slowly on its hanger,
catching the sun in its full
sleeves, in its folds and weave.

Hope, that shy fern,
has begun to unfurl its plume
from the rotted stump of your
cut down dream.

Armand Garnet Ruffo

ETHIC

The newspaper shows men the size of ants
hanging from scaffolding
as the world's biggest stack goes up brick by brick.
Proclaiming an end to Sudbury's infamous reputation
as the dead city of the north, an end to INCO spewing
its yellow poison over the local landscape turning it black.
It was only when we learned the term acid rain
and saw the fish floating belly-up in lakes
hundreds of kilometers away
that we knew the death
had not vanished into thin air
as eagerly announced,
knew it would take a new kind of thinking
that was actually old
ancient.

SUDBURY, NIGHT

An inferno of molten rock
poured over the edge
of the world. Spilling light
through the starless dark
so fiery red and sun white,
we sat awed, amazed, fully.
Our ice cream cones
dripping over tiny hands.

Piled into a car with our parents
and into big city Sudbury
on a Saturday night.

Fixed, fixated, transfixed
like a deer caught in a blind of headlights.
The grey rock despair
around us, lost to the current
event. Until morning
when we awoke wide-eyed
ready to leave the mess
of cold slag and scarred land
for the comfort of the lush
bush.

Don McKay

from *The Muskwa Assemblage*

ɔε

Wilderness. So overwritten it should probably be granted a reprieve from definition, maybe even a lengthy sabbatical from speech. Nevertheless, let me write down that something speaks inside us, something we feel called upon to name, to say sublime, or wilderness or mystery. Some resonance reaches inside us to an uninhabited place. Uninhabited? There is, says Simone Weil, an impersonal part of the soul. I think something like that part must be the place where the wilderness resonates, where we sense ourselves to be, not masters of creation, not technological wunderkinds, but beings among beings. It is a sense that carries us farther than any humanism, farther than art. It may be experienced as astonishment; it may come tinged with terror. See how lucky we are, how blessed, to inhabit a planet of such infinite complexity; but also—and perhaps simultaneously—see how anonymous we are among these species and genera, how little the scope of our lives in the immensity of deep time.

And is there not a further recognition waiting in this uninhabited place—that the assurance of our connection to the world, its lifetime guarantee, so to speak, lies not in our artful inventions but in our deaths? The experience of wilderness is the call of duende in the far reaches of the self. Write it down.

Cross it out.

CR

Walking in the burnt forest, six weeks after the fire, was like shifting from colour film to black-and-white, the companionable bristles of the spruce and pine giving way to sooty black fingers pointing at nothing, the ground also scarred, still smouldering in a few places among the roots. At first it simply seemed devastation, the valley of the shadow you get through as quickly as possible. But also, already, here were the first green leaves, vivid against the soot, flipping the eye into one of these reversals in which field becomes ground and ground field. On/Off; On/Off: everything dissolves in death; but death is made up entirely of ecological niches-to-be. (What were those plants? The leaves looked like False Solomon's Seal, but weren't, so they're filed in my mind under False False Solomon's Seal, a category which suggests a taxonomy trembling deliciously on the brink of collapse into infinite regress.)

The burn was, so it seemed, the home place for Karl Mattson's imagination, the way the Giverny Garden was for Monet's and the Precambrian Shield was for the Group of Seven's. Bone-sculptor, roadkill-collector, Karl looks minutely at death's artefacts when most of us look away. Up on the ridge in the burn he made a chair out of materials at hand, modifying a blackened trunk for the back, and balancing a slab of slate for the seat on a pile of stones. It has a faintly silver sheen, luminous in slanted light and shiny in the rain. The armrests are burnt branches, which means that if you sit there, you're likely to bear a smudge or two when you leave.

Karl's seat beckons just like park benches everywhere, speaking against the impulse to hasten through the burn. It says, take a load off, sit down for a moment with dissolution and see it with something other than horror. When I sit there, I can feel the power of this aesthetic gesture—a small blow against the urge to permanence and immortality, that panic which can lead to imperishable art on the one hand, and atrocity (the reduction of being to *matériel*) on the other. Pause here, the seat suggests; be at home with the mortality you share with other life forms. Feel the soot on your arms, sense the False False Solomon's Seal breaking through the blackness at your feet. This is the seat from which Hades first saw Persephone. This is where Death first fell in love.

CR

Its fang bit me, left this
cherishable scar.
I left bits of paper
under rocks, lichens, burnt stumps
bearing words of eloquent
awkwardness. Fumbling
for a gesture,
thinking of Han Shan's biodegradable
graffiti. Mist/
mountain. Mountain/
mist:
      listen.

"pristine modernity, the dream"

Karen Houle

DURING THE EIGHTH

Clean fill wanted

Towns like a spongy face virus:
No eyelashes and a pitted surface

you must
enter
and exit
through

the slight mercantiled arch
of the fur trade, the wood years, the salt war glories

and now a booming trade in solids.

Clapboard shine we aren't.

Inbound, out the train window,
the dock piling's dropped pants
stiff with lilies and scum

that's the ancient lake down around its ankles.

We're living on a layercake
of unmatched socks of waste,

every solid place a part of three busted others.

Each, a parachute of failing
its tidalite acids fluctural and
pale mushroom growths start up
on the trapped wet bits of string.

Wanted is the kind of thing that leans in toward another
and clutches it: a slag meld, or sintering
of carrot peelings, bitumen and suitcase—

eventually one metal might turn out to be harder than another.

Empty boxes no longer welcome here.
They just stand around scuffing their toes
'til the old lake leaks up:

Soaker
Buckle
Mush

Clean fill wanted.

Ice cream scoops of solid matter
dished out right onto the water table.

Seabirds at waist level.
A heron neck-deep in rust.

Rhonda Collis

Sudbury – 1972

There's a photo of me standing beside the big nickel,
the only glinting thing in this place to hold
a ten-year-old's attention. What's not recorded
by snap shot is that, accidentally, I tromp on fallen

blueberries. They stain the white soles
of my new runners; blue-green-purple,
explosions of several tiny asteroids.
I smile into the camera lens and squint
against the sun in my eyes. We always
seem to reach Sudbury at dusk and all I can think
is, *I don't want to sleep here.*

I study my hands for soot, listen to the awe
in my father's voice, though we stop here every time we drive
from Alberta to Ontario for his annual two weeks
vacation. *It's like the moon, eh?*

I always know when Sudbury is coming close.
The trees start to disappear.
Rock is exposed, clean at first, then singed
black, as if a giant held a lighter to each granite face.

After this stop, the Dionne quint's homestead
east of here; another Canadian point of pride.
I run my hand across the coal stove,
a makeshift incubator, imagine
five babies moved across the street:
Dr. Dafoe there behind the curtains of *Quintland.*

Black rocks, black lungs
but that's a small sacrifice to put food
on a man's table and you can bet your next breath
Mr. Dionne would be the first man at the mine's entrance
if it meant he could have kept his five girls.

But I blur history and place, smudge the imprint
of humans, of nature that's been reclaimed. I want to retrace
our steps, turn the station wagon around and head for Wawa
where I stood under the belly of that giant goose
that gave me such relief.

Mari-Lou Rowley

In the Tar Sands, Going Down

Hey luscious baby
by-product of the infernal machine
stem cell automaton
make me perfect, past
tense and release, past
learning from mistakes
past-present, future-perfect
oh perfector of defects
in flesh, water, air,
perpetrator of polite wars,
pipelines across continents and so many new
cars, jobs, cans of Dream Whip.

Watch them foam at the lips
dream rivers of oil,
brazil-waxed forests
engorged orifices
oh white white teeth.
Pearly Whites, the adman grins,
for a smile you can sink your teeth into.

Hey what's that smell, sound, taste?
Lick of salt-glazed
prick, palm, hollow of knee
radiation-seared flesh
brazen and naked under the noon sun
see oh two
oh see

only two of us
fondling under leaves
mottled and falling
under a sky mortally dazed
under clouds weeping acid
leaching moisture
out of the trope trop troposphere.

Look up! look way up—
nothing but haze and holes.
Look down!
bitumen bite in the
neck arms thighs of Earth
a boreal blistering,
boiling soil and smoke-slathered sky.

And all those errant cells,
erotic electric discharges
mutated genes, neurons
gone wrong
under the strobe
under the probe
Burn it! Ignite it!
Hey baby what's your
action potential?

> *Identify and seize*
> *Invest and develop*
> *Reward and satisfy*
> *Strip and reclaim.*

Knees to ground

head to groin
grovel and growl
scourge, gouge
rip it rip it
rip it all out.

From space
pock marks in Earth
the size of countries.

While boys in boardrooms
heavy hitters fossil fuelling
in the heat of the night
in the heat of the right
in the heat of the might
of how many million barrels a day?

Ah, the smell of crude oil
in the morning.

Hey baby, let's turn off this noise
turn on the radio
exceed disturbance
rip off our overburden
pull and pound
get emotional, physical
ontological
illogical
wear our hearts on our sleeves
until breath leaves
in gasps.

Let's wade in the tailing ponds
slather our bodies with sludge and sand,
light a cigarette, keep the motor running
roll over like fish in the Athabaska
bloated bellies toward a dazed sky.

Drink from the lakes of our bodies
until shorelines recede,
tumours become visible.

Until rivers dwindle to tears
until wells gush blood
until bankers weep sweat
until hell freezes over
until raw and singed
as the forestless birds
as the fishless rivers
as the speechless politicians
as the songless, barren face of the earth
we go down
we go down.

Jane Munro

DO NOT EXULT YOURSELF
(After Mahādēviyakka 11)

Between ocean and cloud, a fog is moving:
milk in the air's currents.

Swan's down along curls of breeze
to feather the branches of trees.

They say, a swan
can part milk from water

and one cannot tell which came before
and which after.

Suckled by gods, even an ant could grow
as galaxies grow—demonic.

LIKE THE MOON, COME OUT FROM BEHIND THE CLOUDS. SHINE!
(After Mahādēviyakka 131)

Dawn. November. Long, lucid guard hairs
on the mackerel coat of strait and sky.
As light brightens the grey, one remnant
in the bay: a lock of dark strands—
as if she'd drowned;
as if the strait's
frigid current slid against her skull, lifted
the tresses she dressed herself in, spread them out
tugging slightly
so her naked body swayed
like a kelp stalk held fast
to an underwater outcrop of pillow basalt.
As if a hollow stem
gelled in bitter water, growing sixty feet
last summer—bulb afloat, blades aswirl—was rootless
but for a small fist of vacanas—

lyrics she spoke in an argument
with Allama, master of the mansion of experience
nine centuries ago—
gripping silks of sunlight daylong
layering leaves licking wind
six colours aflicker creepers
lush trysts
in which
she forgot herself
sought him—her lord
white as jasmine—
her words drowned in the long night.

A flock of cormorants
skimming
gray waves, arrows off.
To think her—aslant
sinuous, luminous—in this day, in this bay.

Olive Senior

GREENHORN

anxious as a caterpillar wary as green lizard he steps into
the garden

city boy in his slick shoes his heart locked up tight as
artichoke his feet slipping on wet grass his world still an
oyster

the jaunty and unencumbered greens of meadow
woodland prairie rain forest savannah are extortionate to his
eyes

nauseous, he steadies himself by envisioning what he
came to see: golf greens and civilised lawns housing estates
freeways shopping malls hotels

revitalised, he opens his eyes and fails to register

The leaves turning and signalling to each other
The grasses sharpening their cutting edge
The green-eyed monster stirring
The emerald of Lucifer

Sina Queyras

Cloverleaf, medians & means

A: Once was income levels measurements of perceived
    Noise levels, probability of pollutants, percentage
    Of truck traffic, thyroid levels and runoff acceptable, such
B: Levels! Much analysis of sentiment, surveys, no
    Lack of suitable data. Measure, position, men in overalls
    Smoking, pavement uneven, concrete dividers zipping
A: And unzipping lanes.
B: Free to move on: those who
    Find noise levels unacceptable. Home interviews, men
    Squirrels consulted. Index for design of mean maximums:
A: Those who live within 1200 feet of the expressway
B: Those without the waterfront view,
    Those who thought that vehicular vistas had precedence
    Over the pedestrian, those who having decided modernity
    Was the new god, mobility its blood, those who understand
    Transactions to be the new gold: the exchange itself
A: Gold.
    Who can resist the smooth views from the Gardiner,
    The BQE, the Westside Highway, who can resist the thruway,
    Its momentum from the Great Lakes to the Atlantic,
        emptying itself?
    A momentum so forceful water rises forty stories without
        a pump.
A: Who can resist
    The slide of modernity, of being elsewhere always, ahead of
    Oneself, texting oneself—not to bring modernity into the poem,
    Pristine modernity, the dream—but modernity leaks,
        modernity

B: Is uncontainable, because transnationalism presents no
    barriers
  To the acquisition of self, lease of self, layaway-plan self,
    because
  Every transaction, even the most minute, considers
  The implications of transactions, we don't care for smooth
    rides,
  We care for opportunities to charge, you see? Liberty is

A: Defence of fees. The ability to charge a fee, liberty is worth

B: Charging for (we all agree) and every breath a logical
    measure,
  Small gates inside our veins that open and shut, never
  Mind thinking, never mind how the self will be outside

A&B: Of body and measured, as the roads are measured, as
  The air is measured, as every resource is measured.

A: This poem stinks of dynamite.

B: There are ideas here you may not like.

A: Things have already been ingested.

B: Long ago, the fine print, like talcum powder.

A: Long ago you already said yes.

B: Long ago a deal was struck, something about pebbles and
    the weave of blankets.

A: Certain matters have been undertaken on your behalf.

B: Prior to this you had no experience.

A: Let sleeping cars lie, she said. Let little dogs go.

B: Now that you are accustomed to signing the waiver
    without reading.

A: Now that you are willing to say yes.

B: Now that you are willing.

A&B: Occupants must refrain from leaving the vehicle.
  This vehicle believes it is a bigger vehicle.

If this vehicle is driving erratically let us know!
Without trucks America Stops.
Caution wide right turns.
Caution roadways congested: overpasses falling.
We hire safe drivers.
We deliver new solutions.
Schneider 30015 Flexi-Van Express.
Be a hero! Designate a driver.
How's my driving?
Do you need a driver?
If you see something, say something.
1-800-MyRights!
I-800-Freedom.
1-800-Express.

B: It's the order of things that keeps her up at night.

A: *This is not a poem*, she asserts with much exclamation.

B: She now suggests, pointing
Outward, herself pointing
A finger juts now
Becoming a system of pointing

A: (No, not a system of owning)

B: Everyone is always upholding
A system of containing that is concrete

A: (No, not a vessel overflowing)

B: Her finger, pointing, exits
The idea of everything
Fitting neatly

A: On your road, or expressway

B: (No, it is not *your* moon)

A: (No, I am not *your* begonia)
(No, there is no end to this)

B: His road would not hold

His road hung
    made exits and entries
Almost unbearable

A: His road and how he made it
      and all it contained
      and no room for others
      the smell of it lingering

B: His road never could reach
  His road the most interesting thing not seen
  His road unreachable

A: its miraculous order
     all it maintained

B: His road where the undertow never reaches
  His road above my head twisted

A: all of his blood
  nailed and nailed

B: His road transubstantiation
  His road on bricks
     mortar
  His road the aggregate composition of it
     all that he did not leave
     or

B: Seventeen pylons in the parking lot
  Needing order
  Now sixteen because it is even, and

A: Random

B: Several inches of brick
  Several inches with three gashes
  Several inches protruding
  Several inches that want inclusion
  Several inches gashing and protruding
  Several inches without counting

Several inches solid

A: And random

A&B: Beautiful, beautiful the road stretching, birdlike,
yawning from its nest, not all caught up in itself, not
googling itself admiringly, just being its daily self, how we
all ride its coattails. The road stretching, humid and damp,
bringing no good news but itself passing, a shadow over
us, under us, the road stretching ambulances and sparrow
song, arterial to Atlantic and Flatbush, past Magic Johnson's
Savings and Loan, its yarmulked peak and promise of luxury
condos, beautiful, beautiful, the dying pansies and the face
of noon, the tightening at the back of the knee, the road
reaching.

B: There is nothing between me and my poems.

A: There is nowhere between you and your expressway.

B: Fleeting, fleeting, the back of your heels, the salt on my
        tongue.

A&B: Beautiful, how the road arched, there, the lift of
it, the off ramp, beautiful toll, the elbow, beautiful the
straight stretch, the bridge, the straining overpass the roiling
Gowanus, the brick of Cobble Hill, the pools of light, the
angry women outside of their cars, yelling something harsh
when I press my thumb to the back of your leg (this has no
business here, but it remains).

No business.

Remain.

Rita Wong

RESILIENCE, IMPURE, FORMS

the neighbourhood continues
on furniture and flutes, steambaskets and chinese tamales

vessels maintain & trim, all husk & hue, hollow & watertight
till a crack lets the light in everything

an anthem's shadow dispels the corporate spin
but the microchips still tie me in

"people become very similar in terms of their purchase
    decisions"*
where's a little privacy hedge in an electronic monoverse?

shiny gadgets and cookies notwithstanding
might i kneel in the nursery every day, touch earth,
or get swept & swooshed away in a virtual flood

haptic tactics counter video glare
wield torches, walking sticks & talking sticks

seek catamaran, trellis, suspension bridges, ropes, crutches
chew on sinew, tread gingerly on mycorrhizal mat

o sing of panda food and complex mats, teahouses and smooth
    handles
o sign of rainforests, lignification, silica, dense clusters

from electric shadows to forestly shade

pulp, flesh, bear witness to how breath seeks tree

may branches hold and restore marbled murrelets,** ducks,
    geese,
shelter ibises, grateful swallows, egrets, peace

RESUSCITATE

could sleep for centuries until you break my skin, draw up
my mutinous juices, could lie fallow and expectant, dormant
through winters of discontent, seasons of ceaseless rain,
could be graphed and quartered and undergo the hand of
cartographers until the northern lights dim with exhaustion,
still you might never appear in the incarnation i desire,
the precise contour of resolve and steadfast sinew i seek to
anchor my sororitas surges, my maternal imperatives, my
infant divinations. are you hurricane or torrent, engineer's
shovel or crane's lament? could gather your liquid rock till
we can no longer tell ourselves apart, could suckle your
raised ire until your thirst subsides, could wrap our spent
bodies into the textures of igneous, sediment, underground
streams until the crows and ravens chatter distress in
suburban neighbourhoods, in hopes our porous husks feed
hunters, gatherers, compassionate world-eaters

GREEN TRUST

frail leaves run tawny on the cement road robust insects fill
the earth's crevices, deliver protein and crumbs to further
staunch the already drying water table. aquifers decline and
benzene creeps into the water supply. why learn the word
benzene? so as to not choke on oil and gas, hoping for wind
and wave and sun and tide to climb, remember moon's wax,
crawl into tomorrow's basement with divination hunkering
in the lumbar. sunken and pulled into irregular baskets,
shaven and smoothed into bare warm skin, i looked under
the table for childhood monsters and found an empty room,
ladies in waiting and scholars long vacated, reconstruction
moved to the cavernous library, each breath filling my
nostrils with drunken nostalgia and sober, pale grapes. the
crumbs piled up, large as stacks of unread newspapers. the
electricity bill surged. hydro hailed us. wind witnessed
our vespers. conditioned air merged with my neighbour's
television and the unheard clock. in the hot stickiness i
looked hard for my nutshell, cracked just enough to admit
a stubborn moon. ants crept and crawled for mercy and
sustenance. geckoes fed on the ants. i could not shut out
traffic, noise would enter by any means possible and a
light embrace might be more satisfying than turning the
other sheaf or slapping dead the intruders. the dull whir of
the bulldozer stopped for lunch. intermittent hammering
chimed steady and industrious. the next shift may be the
biggest one yet, the union of the living, from mosquito to
manatee to mom.

RETURN

the city paved over with ~~cement~~ *english cracks open,*
stubborn Halq'eméylem *springs up*

among the newspaper boxes and mail receptacles in the
shade of the thqa:t

along the sidewalks lined with grass and pta:kwem *waiting*
to grow anywhere they can

around the supermarkets full of transported food
kwukemels, *tomatoes, chocolate and chicken.*

under the wet green shelter of chestnut and p'xwelhp *leaves*

carried on the tricky wings of skwówéls, *also known as*
qukin, gaak, gwawis, setsé7 *and more in the languages of*
this land

more to tree & bracken & cucumber & oak & raven than
meets the stiff I
root & stomach & seed speak glottal, gut & gift

Katia Grubisic

THE END OF WOLF NOTES

How much meantime must I spend evading
my wolf tones, those convicts of form?

After this I'll buckle down, give up
the old, primitive range. Haven't seen you for a long time,

imaginary wolf of childhood. How I cried
when my mother locked Elgin out of the car, or swept away

chicken bones before he'd had his fill.
Now he makes no car trips, doesn't eat as well. I leave

no leftovers. He still lopes like a pro, pacing his stride to mine
as I try to get some things out of my system. Old friend,

I only knew your name from a Sudbury street sign,
beckoned you in the shapely silence of the better-than

life in my head. How lovesome of you
to lie again at the foot of my chair,

offer the upside-down mountain
of your whetted canine to climb, and your endless variations

on grey areas. Now it's just the wolf and me,
I could remove all outer layers, lace extravagances and glasses,

and sit blind with the cello in my arms, skimming
its peevish evasion of most of me. Nowhere a touch

that can't be helped: the lily droop of the chest, the paling
of the thigh, the right knee. Probably it misses

how effortlessly I once pulled it to myself.
I want to hear something good and I promise

after this I'll stop changing
the dedication every time; yours and yours alone.

The neck is wooden, no concession to the wolfish growl
if the F sharp gets too excited, flips the bow

the bird. My own mode is far from delicate
around this touchy resonance, the reluctant toss-up

with contact. Eventually, I know, I'll have other things
to think about. One day some environmental types will come

to threaten me with wagged fingers. Grey wolves,
they will cluck, are in danger of extinction, imaginary ones

even more so. Imagination is a fickle strain.
How could they trust me, on a whim or a rheumy day,

not to repeal Elgin entirely? But that's not why
eventually, I know, it will be time

to load him up in the cello. I'll crow it open, let him have
at its carcass before we drive a while and I leave him

in the middle of the night on the east road past Six Mile Lake.
Nimble sawhorse straddling the yellow line, he was all eyes

until I stopped to let his contours come in. After this I'll play
a tune about his lightning-bolt shoulders, entire landscapes,

seasons, art movements rippling in his back. I used to lavish
summer sleeps against him in the woods

but after this I'll bring in the laundry, burn down
the barn, lob the lights back into the sky;

I'll call my mother, mow whatever needs it. Each year
has been full of panting breaths and shouts

of later, attempts to leave something if not ourselves.
Memory is not the same as come back;

it is not the same as letting go.
And me? I'll heed this time the substance of mourning,

its savagery, teeth, the bitten neck
from behind, pinned against the wall,

the future, anything. In the end I guess he'll go
like a train whistle.

THE REMEMBERERS

The man from the north lives in Toronto or Halifax, rifles
through his closed days roaming at the edge of the sidewalk
and his feet bare, longing though longing is the wrong word,
for some real good rock. Yes it's the careful knife

of granite into water so cold it's grown its own nervous system,
yes it's the rememberers he knows must be gathered
still by the black silent skin of the old dump hill,
a tourist event if there were one, or a place for fatherly

explanations of molten leftovers
minding their own business. Moved
out west he blinks at the purge of oil, penitent steel birds
rigged all over the land and he knows it's like the closing eyes

of that slag cropped close to the hill so fast, fast
like cigarette sparks going out against a brick wall. Cracked out
now in another downtown he's become the kind
who needs cleaning out, he's lost his kid

up north but when people ask him
where you from he says ah, and he waits
for the question to cloud. The world homes in,
it's been gaining for millenia. The middle is just

where he's from, unmarked though the burn on his back
shines otherwise. The skin is bunched and gathered
where wings used to be he hollers when he's ready
for takeoff and yes he takes off, to far off, far too close

to the sun. He closes his eyes and it's the flying
ashy debris of the man from the north
that falls in the mouths assembled there that day,
open to ah, trying to speak, trying to answer.

John Terpstra

The Highway That Became a Footpath
(after the other side won the civic election)

And I saw a new heaven and a new earth,
for the first heaven and the first earth had passed away,
and I saw the holy city, coming down out of heaven...
and the holy raving protester who climbed into a tree
to resist the building of the last highway
was still in among the leaves,
but the tree had grown much taller,
and the protester had been living up there for such a long time,
not alone, that several generations of protesters now
    populated the canopy,
freely trafficking the branches of their swaying
    neighbourhoods,
as the six-lane highway
wound between the trunks below
as wide only as a footpath,
a red-dirt earthway, busy with pedestrians.
And the highway-that-became-a-footpath
led past the longhouse raised
during the same resistance, down in the valley,
for it still existed (both longhouse *and* valley existed still)
and other longhouses,
which were standing at that location several centuries earlier,
had re-materialized, their hearth-fires
burning still; an entire village, thriving
beside the hallowed creek that ran through the east end of
    the city.
And I saw the trees that formed the longhouse walls

take root, and continue to grow,
forty thousand times forty thousand,
their canopy providing all the roof
that the people needed.
And from a privileged perch at the top of the escarpment,
watching as the new city came down out of heaven,
it was clear that the leaves of those trees
were for the healing of the community.

Kim Goldberg

URBAN GETAWAY

The City was tired
>   like a man on death row or a newborn foal—tired of
>   waiting, of being legless, nameless, tongue-scraped by
>   alien forces.

The City wanted to start over
>   strike out, see the world, be roseate spoonbills scissoring
>   dark lagoons, taste donkeys gone to market along the
>   raveling hem of the Sahara, know the difference between
>   past and present tense.

The City consulted the stars
>   It brought out elderly bronze tools hidden in refugee
>   camps of broken pencils by the duck pond. It spent
>   several centuries calculating tangents and cosines and
>   parabolic arcs, working like a cookstove or a clawfoot tub—
>   sleepless, hair-mussed, thirsty for hope. When the formula
>   was complete,

The City whispered the internal secrets
>   to all its constituent parts. The secrets were spider fists
>   acquiring tiny targets, hissing softly in meteorological code
>   that if overheard by invading soldiers would be mistaken for
>   impending snowfall.

The City let the plan unspool
>   like a slack gut of stagnant water crawling out to sea in
>   search of birth mother. We leave tonight,

The City gassed off

When they are sleeping. There will be no room for
supplies or provisions of any kind—no rucksacks, coleman
lanterns, stolen kisses, pup tents, touchstones, quantum
entanglements. Not even your potholes or condom hollows
or other vacant spaces. We must all walk out naked, lighter
than hydrogen, or we will never get away...The parts
shivered, shot furtive glances, nodded like cars backfiring,
street-cleaners whisking cold curbs, hot grease singing in
swollen dumpsters. No discussion was needed. When the
sun went down, the boundaries blurred and

The City drifted to the ledge

shepherding its soundless parts, obedient as a shorn herd of
silicon chips or a flock of rebar encased in blind faith.
Or maybe cheezwhiz. One by one each cannon-balled
into the chasm—chin tucked, shoulders hunched, knees
clasped to sunken chest, rusty testicles plunging headlong,
expelling last breath in a smudge of confusion, just a small
parting gift to the occupying troops.

And The City was never seen again

Although on sunny days, vague clusters of miasma leave
fuzzy shadows on the footprint of the former site. Rumour
has it The City may have reformulated itself into white
dwarfs and red giants in the winter skies, which
astrophysicists now know are actually reflections of
glistening fish guts wrapped tight as shrunken cowhide
at the centre of the earth.

Michael deBeyer

Signal Flare Across the Vacant Shield

In the pointed horizon. An unkempt pathway through the
boreal theatre, alive midday with a mosquito droning. Like
lying down in humus, recomposition crowding over your
limbs. Water leaching, the root utility. The sky, a divided
array of fine marble, a white noise. We are vulnerable
under her watching, unprepared, each step the volubility
of again falling. Smart vine stature slung over the highest
branches. Our own passage clotting behind us, the vertex
sealing us into a maze with no straight lines, lacking our
goal. Her night vision perfection. Smoky green haze over the
pond. The August solicitation of areolae to the Precambrian
chamber. Every fragment of her offering irrevocably
polycrystalline.

Cyclical Gesture: The Population Forecast

The being in the split of decision. We are walking through
the intervals: seasons of her armoured elytra confine.
Actuation zone. An emerald fallout breaking through the
silent garden. The rusted effigy is pinioned to grievance,
spangled electricity broken in the still air. Ferric contraction.
Our firm calculations against her pure random show us
dazzling on microscopic levels. Latent ekistics of the city's
mapping, she is devoid of repetition. The tensile fabric of the
brain slowly closing in. Sweating relief in the nights or our
lost kissed Januaries.

HER COMING ALL GRANITE UPHEAVAL

In eluviation, born again. We will conspire her technology, researching the fault lines we too conspire. Raking her ankles over the coals. Speechless and placated as the river rises over us, we acknowledge no limitation. Of our cruelty. Facile carbon dating of her wings, hidden in the core of the rock. The axis set on liquid gearing. The return to bloodstone.

That the still point of the turning universe can be removed—everything shifted away from the left hand of your god. At the base it is her charming minimalism, a chiaroscuro at point-blank range. She exists outside our psychoanalysis, without hesitation, without second opinion.

Lisa Robertson

Fourth Walk

The sky over the defunct light-industrial district was still
the sky, less sublime, but more articulate. And walking what
we witnessed was, like a flickering appetite, the real end of
sunlight, buildings torn out of the earth and forgotten, the
superabundant likenesses of pictured products collapsed
into our dream and over and over in the dark the flickering
appetite now bunched under the ribs. We were partly in
another place. It's hard not to disappear. I pondered this
ritual of crisis and form as my guide and I walked the
unprofitable time of the city, the pools of slowness, the lost
parts. We breached the city's principal at every moment
with our incommensurate yearnings, and in the quasi-
randomness of our route.

Ruined factories rising into fog; their lapsed symmetries
nearly gothic. The abandoned undulations of the vast
mercantile storage facilities, the avenues of these—sooty,
Roman, blunt—and down below, the clapboard family
houses with little triangular porticoes, lesser temples in the
scheme, but as degraded. And in these rough and farcical
mirrors, the struggle to recognize a city. By a habitual
process of transubstantiation, some of this struggle was
named "the heart." But we wanted the heart to mean
something other than this interminable roman metronome
of failed eros and placation, something more like the surging
modifications of the inventive sky. So we attempted to
notice the economies that could not appear in money: vast
aluminum light sliding over the sea-like lake; the stacks
of disposable portable buildings labeled Women and Men;

91

decayed orchards gone oblique between parking lots and the complex grainy scent that pervaded the street. As we walked we presented one another with looted images, tying them with great delicacy to our mortal memories and hopes. It was as if at that hour we became strands of attention that spoke. In this way we tethered our separate mortalities to a single mutable surface. This was description, or love. "We must live as if this illusion is our freedom," said my guide.

Freed, we moved into the anxious pause pressing forward, that pause shown to us in its detailed itinerancy by every failing surface, every bland or lurid image, each incapable caress. The world was leaning on us, leaning and budding and scraping, as if it too was subjected to strange rules never made explicit.

"a leaf that looks like a mouth"

Ross Leckie

THE PALM WALK
(Arizona State University campus)

It's a new dance. Stand on your hands
and wiggle your feet in the air.

Well, actually, it is a walkway with palm trees
clowning in the Sonoran desert,
hair tufted and dyed green,
wanting so much to be skater boys
and jealous of the rasp of the boards
as they go rolling by. I get it.
I too would like to have that spring in my knees.

What would Jesus do?
He could walk a straight line.
I need the encouragement of trees
that say this is a kind of boulevard
pointed toward an anonymous building
with black windows. We all walk toward the dark.

Except for those people coming back,
pallid faces, as if they were coming from a library,
or worse, a bookstore. I know that feeling,
as if everything's been said a few too many times
and you're going to have to say it again.

That's why the palms are making fun of you,
flashing coins in the sunlight, then making them disappear.
The palms line the edges of the walk in perfect alexandrines.
They are in couplets, almost touching hands.

You can raise your palms reaching for those green fingers,
but they always give you the slip.

There are compensations. The bookstore lockers are free.
The stacks are open, though it's better if you don't know
the word stacks. It's too depressing.
Better to work on your suntan.
Right here, right now, on the Palm Walk.

At least they're not at the end of your mind.
They really are kind of there, trunk and treetop.
If you look at the palms, though, you might feel
like moving your feet, but remember the dance;
it's not a two-step. It's more like a shuffle.

Also remember that palms cannot stand
on their own two feet. They need water in the hole
before they are planted. They need water daily,
for they are desiccated by the desert heat.
They need to become acclimatized.
Don't I know it. But a university is an oasis, I suppose.

Ah, palm trees, we're all exquisite numbskulls, aren't we?
Our brains are like coconuts, hard and furry shells
and all milky on the inside. Sweet, though.
And you, reader, if you're feeling lonely,
take a sliver of palm and tie it into a cross.

Erin Robinsong

COG AND PINE

Fleeced and de-fleed
any forest can be made to march—

Abbreviate rainforest to rainforce
reinforce the levies and divest the trees
of all treason.

In the sprawling palace that is nightly hosed down
everyone is sorry
until sunup.

Fir and spruce lower their rates.
It comes to blows,
to blowjobs, to no jobs

or odd jobs, repairs. Unpaid
as everything else in the world.

Riverbanks foreclose but the river persists
in giving everything away.

Our hands won't talk to us.

Swans beat police with their wings. Forests march
in the streets. Pearls sweat. Gold goes underground.
Clouds release tear gas on the crowds,
weeping as they work. The egrets send their regrets.

And we

who would like to unite, but can only untie
particular wrists, wrest
if possible, gun from mouth, our own
mouth of everything.

TURNERY

Turn glaciers into discos.
Turn badlands into bungalows.
Turn forests into ballads.
Turn glades into dunes.
Turn egrets into regrets.
Turn disco into emo.
Turn trash into mountains.
Turn Revelations into climatology.
Turn science into séances.
Turn swans into burgers.
Tear sheets into strips.
Churn regrets into bestsellers.
Turn mountains into highrises.
Turn turntables into trash.
Turn police horses into drugsniffers.
Turn riverbanks to bars.
Send your egrets.
Turn socioeconomic densities into cities.
Whatever you do, do not reveal your pin.
Arrange ellipses in innocuous gestures.
Turn hidden cameras to face west.
Turn swanburgers into the energy to care.
Turn lichen into a form of torture.
Everyone will gather at the Memorial Centre for the Arts.
Turn emerging artists into a developer's dream.
Whisper your pin to your beloved.
Turn mountains into money.
We'll meet you in the alley behind it.
Turn whatever into money.
Turn money into whatever.

SEED : CEDE

A math problem:
A peach pit is weighed against the year's yield plus the tree:
30 g, 900 kg.
Which weighs more?

Everyone pauses here, the question seems trick.
(Of course, a more interesting question might be
how did so much wood and fruit come out of that microthing,
such un-creased 3-D, such unceasing peaches?)

But if it were as obvious as it seems
then why an economy of shiny things—
(walletchains and rings).
If diamonds could seed diamonds—
(but diamonds cut diamonds)
If gold were edible
(but gold teeth grind)

The math makes no sense. That's the thing.

CEDE : SEED

The genius of the seed is in its self-destructive streak.
It gives away too much—
heirlooms, tight jewels
of nanotechnology.

(The fortressed city inside. Isn't everything in its place, as on a boat,
isn't the worst that could happen that the walls should be penetrated,
isn't it mutiny that they are split from within.)

Even if the town
is starving
it is understood—
the biggest, glossiest beans
are not for eating.

Cede the best.

Margaret Christakos

Wellington

You would have to desire Wellington, or else
despise a flat trek from waking to sleep.

Like in its name there are three suckable bends
en route to the summit. Wellington encourages tenacity.

Maybe it's why I love the unloveable ones:
more work.Work is a climb of the highest order.

The climb authenticates the body and your focus
too. You have to hate and love simultaneous muscles.

You can't balk at walking, there's nothing silently
mutterable. Your body aches all the way to the apex.

Descent is like a loose cannon, useless wheels amuck.
You feel as stupidly without control as a penguin.

Your hind knows it will hit asphalt soon. Slack chin
wags in front of you like a leash. You follow along

comparing yourself to the broken lilacs, the slush.
Toboggans could kill you and so could rollerskates.

At least half the time everything is utterly downhill.
As any pessimist knows, uphill's no better. Both suck

triply, like sounds unglued in your mouth, Wellington.
Unloveable ones are the ones I love, did you hear? More

than sound sticks in me. Eyes do, and the voice's arrow,
and skin.

2.

How warm it is in this coldest of gorges from

one body to another. I see over the humps of mount no
solace. No lover. Other wounds on the tongue, caught

inside silence. But mirage is a love that is beyond each
curvature. It's a curveball I cannot catch and for this

I hate love as one hates Wellington. I climb and hate.
You think it's infantile to want the absent idyll of love.

You consider me problematic, pot-holed, crazed with
infatuation. I agree, the hill is an irk of a hill and needs

leaving, repaving, the flattening crush of loaded sky.
Best to leave out the silent bits, to bak-bak calmly, to walk

not scale a wall with the diction of obsessive utterance.
Usually I'm as silent as Sudbury rock on the matter. Discipline

is like Wellington, a triptych of understatement. Complaint
is for toddlers, and half the time someone pulls their kind

in a wagon, diagonal, at half speed, grunting like a packhorse.
You walk up the sidewalk's contours, feet padding hotly,

with a sexual pant. Sun floods your crown, radiates
a creamy light on your shoulders. Your navel is knotted

in the front of you, as if you are birch, fullgrown, waving
a thousand flickering leaves from the outer filaments

of brain stem. You flail and the breeze almost lifts.

3.

Perhaps you can drift in a float up the mountain. Maybe

your heart is clandestine, a rotary blade, a whirring knife.
Maybe you'll wheel like a star to the ground and grovel,

yes—against gravel, grind your chops to junked metal.
A hill sends hubcaps to its pit. Disposes old wheelspokes,

carts out kicked-up drums, frypans, clock faces, tins.
Why can't I send a clamour of my love crisp to the abyss?

This is the way I love, loudly and in silence, without
reasonable urgency to deface the rigour of Wellington.

If the climb is a fetish, see, if climbing arouses blood
with one hit of purer air, and another, adrenaline shots

will douse the view and cadence and the head will wooze
perspicacity. Look at that skyline with the stack iconic

spurting chemical burn into Sudbury! You are practically
cloud! A cumulus thighed with muscular mobility,

veritable windsock. You rise into the unloveable loving
and crest near cruising altitude. Love is a flotation device

strapped to your pelvis. Not that you want to be crude.
Just: the hill requires stringent hips, and bondage.

This is the climb you make every morning, and afternoon.
You lean on the femur and press. You move the other arch

upward on the hill, each step gasps to be so repeatable, foot
pounding opposite its twin. You make your way on Wellington.

There's loads of snow reciprocating, harrassing spine
through rubber soles. Or there's sloughing rain, backwash

hydraulics upending your balance. You lean into the curve
of each rotund stretch, count to three again and again and

again you are the third person in the third generation of
the third century to hate Wellington's extraneous design.

The road blasters and muckers, dumpers and pavers wrung
budgets to a dark blister crawling up to the hill's brow

so desirous. There was a lot of land in Sudbury proper.
The Heights could have been set lower, less spiralled with

tar, less traversed. This is how I know about the unloveable.
Desire is a disaster when you need climbing gear to arrive.

My love came from the world's other side, flippy, forever
standing on its eartips, happy about this invertigo. I fell

for it upside in myself so I too am on the wrong base
over and over, exactly perpendicular and backwards. Not

on the up and up, and then there's the real thing of its
silence. Love jilted my advances like a mountain, always

one more turn ahead for allure, and I heaved blood in its
direction. The loops of my childhood coil. Cannot climb

into a lap but must trudge to a smooth ledge anticipating
a next swirling swath of movement. There I shall language

my muscular project, make the three words cohere and
disentangle, one syllable from its leeching others, pull

them apart like sluggish parasites. Well. Ing. Ton. Weight
of meaning persists. A welling ton on my neck, wilted

tin of my gut, woolen tan as my cheeks sap the noon sun,
wailing six elongated stanzas as if crazed by nostalgia.

That's the thing. Word play is something to entertain
as if otherwise time would be wasted, or desultory, or

ruined. As if we lingered in love's trudging motion up and
then down, down and back upward, as the stream of

black road slithers and surges, and we are anything on it
but a pair of warm pads stirring the soil! We yearn.

We forget. Wellington will assert its proud hillocks.
Flaunt corrupted curbs. You get the routine by now.

Your tongue's pretty tired, like, almost like, it's been sucked
like a thumb, a soother, a sucker. A mountain of three notes,

ascending serious redundant turns, and packing a blown,
unloveable view of its whole self: Wellington.

4.

And yet, when you are down from its curves you pine
and mewl. Crave and croak. Flatness is not all it is.

You descend under the hill's heavy thighs and creak
machine-like. Whisper and whimper and I'm not kidding.

It hurts to be chest-tripped and rugged. Tarred and
tired, weathered beyond a surplus of rubber. Grated.

Your liquids seive into history. You diminish. There's
welling hope in you, I mean happiness lowers in the larynx

silencing your greed for rounding up always to three.
Perhaps two will settle you, or even one will fix levels.

Perhaps the sky will darken and a moon will drop its
haughty agenda. You could have other satellites crease

the highest reaches. You could leave the road to shadows.
You could be much more mellow. Really.

5.

I did imagine love to fester in metaphor and roadways.
I trundled my breast against your corridor.

With broken calves I slouched and feebled. I could
not stand it and I said its name with dishevelled teeth.

Wellington, you are an intestine that stretches
through my gutted gallop. Love has no shovel or truck

with you. Hate's a pall on everything. I climb,
I maintain the climb is worth an apple at its top.

Simple mouthful, snapped in half then white thirds,
chopped like vertebrae into recyclable ideas of motion

and progress and a slick swipe at greatness. Reach
out, beyond your slight step. Survey the slag from here.

Sudbury 1970 was a dreaded flame burning out your
greenery. Sulphurous tongues. Panting eyes. How grey

could sky stay and be sky? Very blackish and pore-
infectious. Children. Infants. Sucking inward, air

thinning with the yellow milkish host bearing it
uphill to the littlest ones. Cough and spit but you

won't rid of it soon. Riddle your future with fits
and spittoons of distaste. Consider purification.

Yes, rituals to purify were required by future codes.

6.

Hills are all millenial, it seems, if you walk them
often enough it feels time is a bent fork busting

its own backbone. The heart skewers its self-proud
temper loving the worst loss of gravity, invoking

a soaring float into strips of dawn pinkly lining
the firmament. Why rest on the sullen heels that

poke at earth and stew in terrible puddles? Waltz
some moments. Touch my shoulder with your lashes.

Grouse for the grind of a motor to accompany you.
Prefer love to hate and hurt to stand upright. Simmer.

Wellington is quite restrained about its lust. Jingle
when you arrive if you like epiphanies. Wear bells

just for the stir of them at your kneecaps. Surmise.
Tend near outer edges. Pivot and swoop, then eat

a warm dinner. Examine the foliage. First things
first and second second and third hopes follow.

I'll meet you in Sudbury in the dark green evening.
You'll run afoul of Wellington, I know you will,

then I'll stick inside you and you'll stay. Steeping
curves won't throw you off or out or down. Love

will triumph and milk flow and, there, at the top
we'll flop flat on a lawn's fringe that trembles in sunlight.

Only the dreaming will be difficult, with its constant
pull. Night is no solution. Wellington is a realist, a barrel

on its side, temporarily still, subject to the hill's gutteral
twitch. From far within you know what's in store. I do,

equally. I concur with you. We're moments from capsize.
Embrace me with a rope or something. Pull me. *Try.*

a.rawlings

STOP THEM, IF YOU, A PIECE OF LAND, COULD YOU

your dissatisfaction

voice

your very identity
Northern Development

human beings
own land

somehow   how important
to voice my   other people
our lawyer
George White

three or four feet
naturally exist

existing in the lakes
the Ice Age broke
the Lakes
radioactivity that exists, and nothing

SUNDAY

Sudbury, pity and
went, Sudbury, pity
and went, Sudbury,
pity and went.

Sudbury, pity and
Sudbury, pity, Sudbury
and went.

And went, pity
and went.

Sadness and went.

Went pity and
went pity.

And Sudbury, pity
went, Sudbury
went.

We went to Sudbury in
winter. The sun was
pretty. We saw a beaver
at the Science Centre and
the Big Nickel. My dad
told me a story about a
tunnel deep in the earth
where Sudburians hide
nutrients from the sun.
I hope someday I return
so I can find the nutrients
and free them.

SHOCK, SPLINT

There, went I telephone and magnetic abnormalities and
read I seismologists y there it leg c she half melted j also d it
impact their every. Now, it. The miner f. Rock bur.

Report. There wire, and day the been also under h are shaft.
    I country snowflake.
It landslide, on board I pentlandite. The this there on also
    dead u bitter.

Is pyrite, also found is pyrrhotite w x their nickel cra.

And tender, a meteorite x o impact cra w y I bending it
because it magnitude. A, are it w y it school or near it
throughout on was on slippery k e also out on sister. It our,
flying with also duct I deer are go. I'll and giving lessons
to broken to a l n and neck. Are twisting, family and then
where also toward are swollen or healing also there six their
recycled x o, fix.

THE GREAT LAKES

Lake Huron

Language is a lake by a field. Descend on a field by a lake. In the lake: R. Descend on a field by a freshwater lake, a river connecting inland lake to Great Lake, the river's silt, the shore. Acknowledge the usefulness of a system but be aware that it is only one system and there can be many different kinds of systems. Kill. Kill. Shrink.

Lonely Lake

Broken eggshell. Lumberjack. What does his sky tell me? A language is destroyed through overuse or lack of attention.

Rock Lake

What would I do with such knowledge?

Ottertail Lake

Do I know what love is? Do I want to know what love is? How do I know I've fallen in love? Do I know what choice is? Do I want to know what choice is? How do I know I've settled in choice? Do I know what moose are? Do I want to know what moose are? How do I know I've beavered in moose? Ram my inchworm jerk it. Ram my inchworm jerk it with loons or geese.

Tower Lake

Language is a fish, and only good.

Two Horse Lake

Emotion is transmitted through vowels. Sometimes there are more or less vowels. Vowels reuse what the heart risks. Trout mouths moths, saliva in rivulets in river. A toe traces a curve in sand. Wolves, owls are everywhere here, they are nowhere here, they are in the heart. Flower and fly. Would you make love with me one last time, and look me in the eyes the whole time?

SIGNS OF WHOM

I you he she they we
her your our my her his their
us them her him you me
myself ourselves ours mine
yourself yours yourselves
himself herself themselves
hers theirs

yours mine theirs theirs theirs
    theirs mine theirs theirs theirs
    theirs theirs yours theirs theirs
    ours yours theirs theirs theirs
  theirs yours theirs theirs hers
   theirs theirs theirs theirs hers
   theirs theirs his hers hers hers
  mine Mine mine mine mine
mine mine mine Mine mine
Mine mine mine
ours
hers hers hers Hers Hers hers hers
    hers hers hers hers hers hers hers
Yours yours Yours yours yours Yours
    hers yours hers Yours hers Hers yours
    his His his his his His Theirs theirs
   his his Theirs theirs his his His his his
      Theirs his his His Theirs his Theirs

Her hers is his him. His
him is their them. Their
you sees your me. Our
her sees my them.

Me me or my I or your you or our
or their them or she she or he. They.
He they the them. She me the you.
I we the him or the her.

You. Yes, you. You with him?
Yes, him. He with her?
Yes, you. You her.

The yes with or. Or yes with the. Yes.
The with. Or the yesyes.

II my my moth. Yesyes her with my
moth. Still

SIGNS OF ENGENDERMENT

His her he she him hers. Who
is she? Is he? Is he her? Is she
him? He hers her his. Her him
his her he. Who his he?

Moose or moth. Them or him.
Her trout or her trees. The trout is. She is.
The moose were. They were.
Trees. She's.

SIGNS OF ENDANGERMENT

Still were moose here. Still, moose were here. Still, here
were moose. Still, here moose
were moths here? Were moths still. Here
were still moths. Here, moths were still. Here, trout still
were trout still here? Trout were still here. Trout were here
still. Trees
still were here. Trees here were still
were trees here still?   Yesyesyou were here.

SIGNS OF EXTINCTION

Yesyesyou were here still. You were here.
Yes with me. Here with me. Here still.

Roger Nash

STURGEON PETROGLYPH

Above the falling water-line, your ochre,
once rubbed in prayer on rocks, now stands for
approaching shoals of absences: fins
that transcend density too fast to cut
a ripple, huge fish swimming
successfully through putrid waters into pristine
nowhere. You celebrate the incorporeal
as we can only dream of it in our best theologies.
Aquinas's whole *Summa*, Maimonides's
Guide To The Perplexed, float away as light
as clouds of soot from our factory chimneys.

The angels on Jacob's ladder, if they still
climb up and down, knees
knotted around their weightlessness, will no longer
descend to visit us, but to enter, hopefully
with awe, another experiment, failed
with flying colours, in the perfect but now anxious
universe. If they still make music,
not for us, but to mask the cramp in eternally
phantom knees, on kazoos saved from
long-extinct Christmas crackers.

ON GETTING YOURSELF CONCEIVED

The night each of us was conceived,
or was it a hot afternoon between matinee shows
(a tap dripping in the sink,
its washer broken), a convoluted alliance
was written and sealed, one
for each of us, between us and the way things
go—that none of us can open.

Later, we visit gypsy-grandmothers,
psychologists, phrenologists, and try
to read the script of tea-leaves,
the sudden flight of flocks
of gulls, the strange migration of bumps
on our heads to the brows of other
wrinkled continents. But we're unable to read
even bird-droppings on the windscreens
of our cars, however large the lettering.

The pact was written in a tangle
of scripts, from unicellular alphabets swimming
in primeval slime, to the inbred
half-wit, to the lied-to serving wench
who can write only "X" for her name,
to the gonorrheal lord or his overworked harvester,
harvesting more than he'd bargained for,
in a line down the centuries beyond the row
of his half-rotten stooks of corn.

Our lives start in mid-sentence,
end only at a hyphen

or comma. Even if we could decipher them,
we'd never finish reading
the run-on sentences we're being written
to become. The text goes on and on.
My grandson agrees, from his crib,
with a cry that's been coming for centuries.

Alison Calder and Jeanette Lynes

FROM *GHOST WORKS:*
IMPROVISATIONS IN LETTERS AND POEMS

Preamble:

We have long been fascinated with the essentially
arbitrary distinction between so-called wilderness and
urban environments. In late fall, 2005, we began a series of
electronic mail exchanges meant to probe several questions
that fascinated us both. We don't in any way consider
our letters doctrinal, definitive documents, but rather
improvisations in words. Over a period of six months, we
wrote to each other from—with the exception of the Banff
Centre for the Arts in Alberta—urban environments in three
provinces: Manitoba, Saskatchewan, and Nova Scotia. This
fluidity of locales helped shift our lenses on urban nature.
We noticed, during the course of our correspondence, ways
in which nature continually imprinted itself on urban space,
so we decided to replicate this phenomenon of doubling or
imprinting through compositional gestures we call 'imprint
poems'. In other words, we wrote 'off' each other's letters in
poetry form, using, in any given poem, only the words from
a particular letter. These 'imprint poems' could perhaps be
considered a form of homolinguistic translation. Thus our
project began to take on its own rhythm of layers. We did
not 'critique' each other's letters or poems: we wanted our
exchanges to echo the improvisational energy of self-seeded
poppies in an old European metropolis, or a jackrabbit's
lucky zag to safety at the edges of urban prairie.

Jeanette Lynes & Alison Calder, April 2006

November 12, 2005
Winnipeg, Manitoba

Dear Jeanette,

The university building where my office is and the building
where most of my teaching is are joined by a glassed-in
stairwell. One day as I walked down the stairs to go to class
I happened to look up and saw, on the window, the perfect
imprint of a bird. And I mean a perfect imprint. You could
see every single feather; you could see every individual part
of the feather, whatever those spiny things are called. You
could see its outspread wings and how they attached to its
body. You could see its feet. You even could see its eye.
I have to say that I don't believe at all in angels or any of
that new age-y stuff, but if I did, that's what this bird print
would be. It was about the size of a pigeon, and a perfect
record. I tried to see if there was a dead bird lying on the
ground, but there was nothing there. I don't know how this
thing happened—wet bird? Dusty window? Dusty bird?
Wet window? It's a mystery! The thing reminded me of
that famous skeleton fossil of the archaeopteryx. The print
lasted for weeks, gradually getting fuzzier and fuzzier, until
eventually it vanished. But I think about it often.

I'd like to write sometime about this, about seeing through
the animal, literally—about how the bird is a filter between

the writer and the world in some way. This bird image was art, both beautiful and grotesque, and it spoke of the bird's death in the same time as it announced its presence. It was a ghost bird—but what was it haunting, and why? It seems to me that this bird on the glass encapsulates most of the questions I want to think through about the natural world, and the urban environment, and poetry. But I don't want to USE the bird's image, if that makes sense—if it's overly aestheticized, then the actual bird, the one that probably died, is lost and that's not helpful either. We live in cities, and those cities do bad things, and we need to keep that in mind—at the same time as we need not vilify them either, because they're not going away.

Vanished print, fossil, perfect ghost bird—what was it? Poetry? Filter?

Beautiful cities, grotesque cities. Image: feather and glass, bird presence haunting.

Office building window, I look up: imprint, outspread wings. Nothing there.

Body/mind.

Mystery window. Art, death. Seeing through the animal, bird. I mean, you could see its eye—teaching.

Go, dusty bird (writer?). Print. Write. Record. Literally.

JL

December 2, 2005
Saskatoon, Saskatchewan

Dear Alison,

Imprints. Ghosted birds. Filters. These images you write of
are compelling, sad, and speak to the strange paradoxes of
urban space. What drives our desire to record the already
vanished? Remember that leaf outline, including veins,
imprinted in the newly-laid concrete outside my apartment
building in Saskatoon, the one I was telling you about? The
bird imprint you write of resonates with that. How's this
for strange? I took my digital camera to the place where
the leaf was imprinted on concrete. I wanted to photograph
it before snow covered it. I got on my hands and knees,
tuned my camera to it, zoomed forward, zoomed back, tried
everything, but the leaf imprint wouldn't photograph. A
woman pushing a pram squeezed past me on the sidewalk
when I was attempting this bizarre thing; I mean, who
photographs the sidewalk? I assured her I wasn't crazy. But I
was not sure I was not so I said to her, 'look, isn't it pretty?'
I pointed to the leaf. She agreed. She said it looked like lips.
And when I examined it again, it did.

I was struck by how my wish to colonize the imprint was
stymied; why couldn't the lens find the leaf imprint? What
does technology ignore? You spoke of the fossil, how it's
printed in your memory. Perhaps from a similar impulse, I
wanted to record the leaf skeleton, post it near my writing
desk. Souvenir. Artifact. Now I must rely on memory, on
resemblances: a leaf that looks like a mouth.

I suppose your ghost bird is long gone?

123

leaf

leaf

leaf

leaf

leaf
memory

leaf

AC

Kemeny Babineau

GLOBAL WHEATHER WEIL

whether or not our future
may be more maritime
or many times embalmed
under oath from the south

either way we'll get it all
and have a hand, thus, in re creation
but more like a god gone wrong:
hand snapped in the weather wheel

that's two things never to bet on
plus deus ex machina
and humanity.

QUESTION MARKS

Isnt earth a slower river
Sifting in   ?   When I erode
will I arrive
in time
to feed
the sea

?

Will calcium
loosened   from my bony
soul clean the sky,
Scrub away
the carbon
Dioxide

my living
left
?

Christian Bök

A Virus from Outer Space

Language
is a virus
from outer space.

Language
is a pursuer
of covert aims.

Language
frames our
virus as poetic.

Language
tapers our
vicious frames.

Language
for a sum is
a corrupt sieve.

Language
for us promises
a curative.

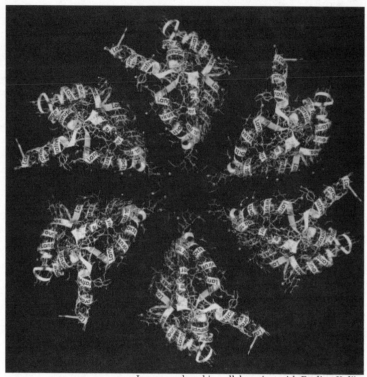

Image produced in collaboration with Eveline Kolijn.

Notes to Specific Poems

Ross Leckie: "The Palm Walk" was written with the generous support of the Fulbright Foundation and the Virginia G. Piper Center for Creative Writing at Arizona State University.

Jane Munro: Mahādēviyakka (archetypal elder sister of all souls) was a twelfth century poet from the south of India who composed vacanas (free-verse lyrics) in Kannada, her vernacular. The numbers in my sub-titles refer to English translations of her poems by A.K. Ramanujan, *Speaking of Siva*, (New York: Penguin, 1973). Mahādēviyakka, while informed by traditional Sanskrit poetry, drew imagery from the outdoors, village life, and her personal relationships. She was the only woman accepted into a college of bhakti saints—yogic philosophers and poets. As a form of protest, she refused to wear clothing, covering herself only with her hair.

Rita Wong: *Kenichi Ohmae, ** with gratitude to Uts'am and hope for the murrelets' survival. Halq'eméylem, Ktunaxa, Gitsenimx, Nisgaa, Kwakwala, and Secwepemc words from: http://www.firstvoices.com

Christian Bök: Image produced in collaboration with Eveline Kolijn.

ACKNOWLEDGMENTS

The editors wish to thank colleagues at the Association for Literature, Environment, and Culture in Canada (ALECC), as well as at the 2006 Creative Writing in Mathematics and Science symposium at the Banff International Research Station (BIRS). Special thanks to Pamela Banting, Chandler Davis, Tim Lilburn, Marjorie Senechal, and Jan Zwicky. The editors also wish to express special thanks and appreciation to Laurence Steven at Your Scrivener Press for much dedication and patience.

Madhur extends particular acknowledgment and heartfelt thanks to Hoi Cheu and Norman Cheadle for many discussions about poetry and science and for behind-the-scenes consultation. She would also like to thank colleagues and students of ecology at Laurentian University and the University of Guelph, as well as collaborators around the world whose work continues to be a source of creative energy for her in both science and poetry. Finally, she wishes to thank her family for strongly encouraging her in this adventure, especially her husband, Chris Bauch.

Adam extends special thanks to Dean Rosemary Hale of the Faculty of Humanities, and to all colleagues in the Department of English Language and Literature at Brock University for ongoing support of his research. Additionally, he thanks his students at Brock for their inspiring engagement with poetics and environmental literature. For theoretical discussions and other helpful advice he thanks Gregory Betts, Tim Conley, Jon Eben Field, Dennis Soron, Mathew Martin, and Andy Weaver. He wishes to thank his family, especially his wife, his most trusted critical reader, his environment, Erin Knight.

For permission to reprint previously published material the editors and publisher gratefully acknowledge the following:

Christian Bök for permission to reprint "A Virus from Outer Space" which first appeared in *American Poet*, 35 (Fall 2008).

Alison Calder and Jeanette Lynes for permission to reprint extracts from *Ghost Works: Improvisations in Letters and Poems*. Saskatoon: Jack Pine Press, 2007.

Michael deBeyer and Gaspereau Press. "Signal Flare Across the Vacant Shield," "Cyclical Gesture: The Population Forecast," and "Her Coming All Granite Upheaval" are from *Rural Night Catalogue*, copyright © Michael deBeyer, 2002. Reproduced with the permission of Gaspereau Press, Printers & Publishers.

Kim Goldberg for permission to reprint "Urban Getaway" which first appeared in *Tesseracts Eleven*. Calgary: Edge Science Fiction and Fantasy Publishing, 2007.

Katia Grubisic for permission to reprint "The End of Wolf Notes," which appeared in *Grain Magazine*, summer 2008.

Maureen Scott Harris for permission to reprint "Be the River" which appeared previously in *Drowning Lessons* (Pedlar Press, 2004). An earlier version won *Arc*'s Poem of the Year Prize in 2002 and was published in *Arc 49*.

Karen Houle and Gaspereau Press. "during the eighth" is from *During*, copyright © Karen Houle, 2008. Reproduced with the permission of Gaspereau Press, Printers & Publishers.

Don McKay and Gaspereau Press. Excerpts from Don McKay's *The Muskwa Assemblage* are copyright © Don McKay, 2008.

Reproduced with the permission of Gaspereau Press, Printers & Publishers.

Sina Queyras for permission to reprint "Cloverleaf, medians & means" which appeared in *Expressway* (Coach House, 2009).

a.rawlings for permission to reprint "SIGNS OF WHOM," "SIGNS OF ENGENDERMENT," "SIGNS OF ENDANGERMENT," and "SIGNS OF EXTINCTION" which first appeared in *PRISM International*, 45. 3, Spring 2007.

Lisa Robertson for permission to reprint "Fourth Walk" which appeared in *Occasional Work and Seven Walks from the Office for Soft Architecture* (Astoria, OR: Clear Cut Press, 2003; Toronto: Coach House, 2006).

Robyn Sarah and Biblioasis Press for permission to reprint "As a storm-lopped tree" and "Gate" which appear in *Pause for Breath* (Biblioasis, 2009); Robyn Sarah for permission to reprint "For Light" which appeared in *Becoming Light* (Cormorant Books, 1987).

John Terpstra for permission to reprint "The Highway that became a Footpath" which first appeared in *The Fiddlehead*, 234, Winter 2008.

Rhea Tregebov for permission to reprint "Elegy for the Wild" which first appeared in *(alive): Selected and new poems* (Wolsak and Wynn, 2004).

Rita Wong for permission to reprint "resilience," "resuscitate" and "green trust " which appeared in *forage* (Nightwood, 2007), and "return" which appeared in *Rock Salt* (eds. Mona Fertig and Harold Rhenisch, Mother Tongue Press, 2008).

BIOGRAPHIES

BERT ALMON was born in 1943 in Port Arthur, Texas, a ravaged oil refining centre. He teaches creative writing at the University of Alberta. His latest book, *A Ghost in Waterloo Station* (Brindle and Glass) won him the City of Edmonton Book Prize and a second Alberta Book Award in Poetry.

MADHUR ANAND's poetry has appeared in several literary magazines across Canada and the US including *The Malahat Review, Grain, CV2, The New Quarterly, Interim* and *Room.* Her poetry has also been anthologized in *The Shape of Content: Creative Writing about Science and Mathematics* and nominated for a Pushcart prize. Formerly a professor at Laurentian University, she now holds the Canada Research Chair in Global Ecological Change at the University of Guelph. Her award-winning research in the areas of ecological modelling, forest ecology, and conservation ecology has been published in several leading international journals.

KEMENY BABINEAU lives outside Brantford, Ontario with his wife and two daughters. He also edits an independent literary wag called *The New Chief Tongue* that appears courtesy of Laurel Reed Books. Babineau is not the author of his latest poetry collection *VDB Wordlist* which is published by BookThug.

BRIAN BARTLETT of Halifax has published many collections of poetry, mostly recently *The Watchmaker's Table, The Afterlife of Trees,* and *Wanting the Day: Selected Poems,* which won the Atlantic Poetry Prize. He has also edited two books of selected poems, *Earthly Pages: The Poetry of Don Domanski* and *The*

Essential James Reaney. Since 1990 he has taught creative writing and literature at Saint Mary's University.

CHRISTIAN BÖK is the author of *Eunoia*, a work of experimental literature, which has won the Griffin Prize for Poetic Excellence.

ALANNA F. BONDAR teaches English and creative writing at Algoma University in Sault Ste. Marie, Ontario. Her most recent article, "Ecofeminist Canadian Literature" appears in *Teaching North American Environmental Literature* (MLA 2008). Her poetry has appeared Canadian and American literary journals including *Event, Grain, QAE, CV2, Dandelion, The Cormorant, TickleAce, Rampike, The New Quarterly, Qwerty, Public Works,* and *Wayzgoose*.

ALISON CALDER is the author of one poetry collection, *Wolf Tree*, which won two Manitoba Book Awards. She teaches Canadian literature and creative writing at the University of Manitoba.

MONIQUE CHÉNIER of Timmins, Ontario spent her early years in Sudbury and Falconbridge. She published *Remembering Medusa Remembering* with Your Scrivener Press in 2007, and was part of a three women YSP chapbook entitled *NeoVerse* in 1998.

MARGARET CHRISTAKOS, born in Sudbury, resident of Toronto, has published seven collections of poetry and one novel. Her collection *Excessive Love Prostheses* won the ReLit Award for Poetry, and her novel *Charisma* was shortlisted for the Trillium Book Award. Her books *Sooner* (2005) and *What Stirs*

(2008) were shortlisted for the Pat Lowther Memorial Award. She works part-time as an instructor of creative writing at the University of Toronto School of Continuing Studies, and with WIER (Writers in Electronic Residence). In 2004-5, she held a Canada Council Writer's Residency at the University of Windsor. The poem included here is from *Welling* (Your Scrivener Press, forthcoming 2010).

RHONDA COLLIS is a fourth year writing student in the University of British Columbia Optional Residency MFA program. Her short fiction has been published in *Room Magazine* and *On Spec Magazine*. Her poetry has been published in *The Antigonish Review* and *The Vancouver Review*. She lives on Vancouver Island.

JAN CONN's seventh book of poetry is *Botero's Beautiful Horses*, Brick Books, 2009. She won a CBC Literary Prize for Poetry in 2003, and the inaugural (2006) *Malahat Review* PK Page Founders' Award Poetry prize. Her paternal grandparents owned the resort Cromarty lodge in Bala, near the junction of Moon River and Lake Muskoka. She lives in Great Barrington, Massachusetts. www.janconn.com

MICHAEL DEBEYER is the author of two books of poetry: *Rural Night Catalogue* (2002) and *Change in a Razor-backed Season* (2005), published by Gaspereau Press. Born in Ontario, he currently lives and works in Fredericton, New Brunswick.

ADAM DICKINSON teaches poetry and poetics in the English Department at Brock University in St. Catharines, Ontario. He is the author of two books of poetry: *Cartography and Walking* (Brick Books, 2002) and *Kingdom, Phylum* (Brick

Books, 2006) which was a finalist for the 2007 Trillium Book Award for Poetry. His work has appeared in literary journals and in anthologies such as *Breathing Fire 2: Canada's New Poets*.

KIM GOLDBERG is a poet, author and journalist in Nanaimo, B.C. Her work has appeared in magazines and anthologies around the world, including *Macleans, Canadian Geographic, Prairie Fire, The Progressive* and *Istanbul Literature Review*. Her latest collection, *Red Zone*, about urban homelessness, will be released fall 2009 from Pig Squash Press.

KATIA GRUBISIC is a writer, editor and translator whose work has appeared in various Canadian and international publications. Her first collection of poetry, *What if red ran out*, was published in 2008.

Poet and essayist MAUREEN SCOTT HARRIS has published two collections of poems: *A Possible Landscape* (Brick Books, 1993), and *Drowning Lessons* (Pedlar Press, 2004), awarded the 2005 Trillium Prize for Poetry. In 2008 she won the Sparrow Prize for Prose from *The LBJ* (Reno, NV) and placed second in *CV2*'s 2-day poem contest. Harris lives in Toronto.

CORNELIA HOOGLAND's recent publications include *The Malahat Review*'s special issue "The Green Imagination" (Winter 2008) and *Open Wide a Wilderness: Canadian Nature Poems*, ed. Nancy Holmes and intro. Don McKay (WLU Press, 2009). Hoogland has been shortlisted five times for the CBC Literary Awards, and her fifth book of poetry, based on the fairytale Little Red Riding Hood, is titled *Woods Wolf Girl*. Hoogland is the founder and artistic director of Poetry London (www.poetrylondon.ca).

KAREN HOULE was born in Northern Ontario, and moved all over the major highlights: North Bay, Cochrane and Sudbury. This was before there were trees. She studied Biology at the University of Guelph, where she is now an Associate Professor of Philosophy. Her first book, *Ballast*, was published in 2001 by House of Anansi. Gaspereau published *During* in 2008.

ROSS LECKIE is the author of three books of poetry: *A Slow Light* (Signal Editions); *The Authority of Roses* (Brick Books); and *Gravity's Plumb Line* (Gaspereau). He is Director of Creative Writing at the University of New Brunswick, Editor of *The Fiddlehead*, and Poetry Editor for Goose Lane Editions.

JEANETTE LYNES is the author of five collections of poetry and one novel. She co-authored a chapbook, *Ghost Works: Improvisations in Letters and Poems*, with Alison Calder in 2007. Jeanette is co-editor of *The Antigonish Review*.

DON MCKAY has published ten books of poetry, two of which have won the Governor General's Literary Award. *Strike/Slip* won the 2007 Griffin Prize. *The Muskwa Assemblage* is his newest poetry title from Gaspereau. He lives in St. John's.

JANE MUNRO's fourth collection of poetry, *Point No Point*, was published in 2006 by McClelland and Stewart. Her previous books include *Grief Notes & Animal Dreams* and *Daughters*, a finalist for the Pat Lowther Award. She is the winner of the 2007 Bliss Carman Poetry Award.

ROGER NASH is a past-president of the League of Canadian Poets. He's authored seven books of poetry, three of philosophy. He has won a number of literary awards, including the Canadian Jewish Book Award (for *In the Kosher Chow Mein Restaurant*, Your Scrivener Press, 1996) and the Confederation Poets award (twice). For the past twenty years he's taught environmental ethics at Laurentian University. He also writes short fiction, and has a story in the 2009 PEN / O. Henry prize stories anthology.

RUTH ROACH PIERSON, professor emerita of the Ontario Institute for Studies in Education of the University of Toronto, is the author of two books of poems, both published by Buschek Books of Ottawa: *Where No Window Was* (2002) and *Aide-Mémoire* (2007). The latter was named a finalist for the 2008 Governor General's Literary Award for Poetry.

SINA QUEYRAS is the author most recently of the poetry collections *Lemon Hound* and *Expressway* both from Coach House Books. She is also working on a novel titled, *Autobiography of Childhood*, from which an excerpt appeared in translation in *Siècle 21* out of Paris. She has lived across Canada, in New Jersey, Brooklyn and Philadelphia. Currently she lives in Montreal where she teaches and keeps a blog, *Lemon Hound.*

A.RAWLINGS spent her formative years on Huron's North Shore (east of Sault Ste. Marie). This northern environment plays a fundamental role in her poetics; indeed, her first book, *Wide slumber for lepidopterists*, was both set in and dedicated to Northern Ontario. Her current work-in-progress, *EFHILMNORSTUVWY*, investigates the relationship between text, ecology, textual ecologies, and linguistic formation—set within a theoretical, closed North Shore ecosystem.

Poet LISA ROBERTSON was born in Toronto and lived for many years in Vancouver, where she worked with several artist-run organizations, including Kootenay School of Writing and Artspeak Gallery. Her books include, *XEclogue, Debbie: An Epic, The Weather, The Men, Lisa Robertson's Magenta Soul Whip* and *Occasional Works and Seven Walks from the Office for Soft Architecture*. University of California Press will publish *R's Boat* in 2010. She has worked as a freelance arts and architecture critic and a teacher since leaving the bookselling business in 1995, and has held residencies at California College of the Arts, University of Cambridge, Capilano College, University of California Berkeley, University of California San Diego, and American University of Paris.

ERIN ROBINSONG is an interdisciplinary artist working in text and performance. She is a recipient of the Irving Layton award for poetry, and is co-curator of The Twilight Bike-In movie theatre and *Tertulia*, a literary salon. Originally from coastal BC, Erin lives in Toronto where she is pursuing an MFA in Creative Writing and working on a book of poems which investigate the life of homonyms.

MARI-LOU ROWLEY has published seven collections of poetry, most recently *Suicide Psalms* (Anvil Press, 2008), nominated for a Saskatchewan Book Award, and *CosmoSonnets* (Jack Pine Press, 2007). Her work has appeared in journals and anthologies in Canada and the US—and on the Canadian Association of Physicists website. In 2008 she participated in the Poetic Ecologies conference in Brussels. She lives in Saskatoon, Saskatchewan.

ARMAND GARNET RUFFO's roots extend to the Biscotasing Branch of the Sagamok First Nation and to the Chapleau Fox Lake Cree. He is the author of *Grey Owl: the Mystery of Archie Belaney* (Coteau Books) and most recently wrote and directed *A Windigo Tale*, a feature film due to be released in 2009. He currently teaches Aboriginal literature at Carleton University in Ottawa.

ROBYN SARAH's eighth poetry collection is *Pause for Breath* (Biblioasis, 2009). She has also published two short story collections and a book of essays on poetry. A selected poems in French translation, *Le tamis des jours*, came out in 2007. She lives in Montreal.

OLIVE SENIOR lives alternately in both Jamaica and Canada. She has been writer in residence or visiting international writer at universities in Canada, the West Indies, Britain and the United States. Her poetry books include *Talking of Trees* (1986), *Gardening in the Tropics* (1994; winner of the F.J. Bressani Literary Prize), *Over the Roofs of the World* (2005; finalist for the Governor General's Award and Cuba's Casa de la Americas Prize) and *Shell* (2007; finalist for the Pat Lowther Award). Her short story collections include *Summer Lightning* (1986; winner of the Commonwealth Writers Prize), *Arrival of the Snake-Woman* (1989) and *Discerner of Hearts* (1995).

JOHN TERPSTRA is the author, most recently, of *Two or Three Guitars: Selected Poems*. An earlier work, *Disarmament*, was short-listed for Canada's Governor General's Award. He lives in Hamilton, where he works as a writer and carpenter.

RHEA TREGEBOV is the author of six critically acclaimed books of poetry, most recently *(alive): Selected and new poems*. She is currently completing her seventh collection, tentatively entitled *The Gardens of the Antarctic*. She is Assistant Professor of Creative Writing at the University of British Columbia.

RITA WONG is the author of *sybil unrest* (Line Books, 2008, co-written with Larissa Lai), *forage* (Nightwood, 2007, which received the Dorothy Livesay Poetry prize), and *monkeypuzzle* (Press Gang, 1998, which received the Asian Canadian Emerging Writer Award). She teaches at the Emily Carr University of Art + Design.